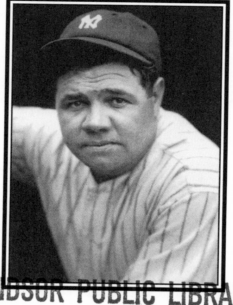

Babe Ruth

Sultan of Swat

Lois P. Nicholson

Goodwood Press
Woodbury, Connecticut

Babe Ruth

Sultan of Swat

Published by Goodwood Press
P.O. Box 942
Woodbury, CT 06798

Designed by Bob Moon,
SporTradition Publications
798 Linworth Rd. E.   Columbus, OH 43235

Printed and manufactured in the United States of America by
BookCrafters, Chelsea, Michigan

Nicholson, Lois, 1949-
    Babe Ruth : sultan of swat / Lois P. Nicholson.
    p. cm.
    Includes bibliographical references and index.
    ISBN 0-9625427-1-7

    1. Ruth, Babe, 1895-1948--Juvenile literature.
    2. Baseball players--United States--Biography--Juvenile
literature. 3. Ruth, Babe, 1895-1948. 4. Baseball players. I. Title.

GV865.R8N53 1995   796.357'092
                                    QBI94-21241

Contents

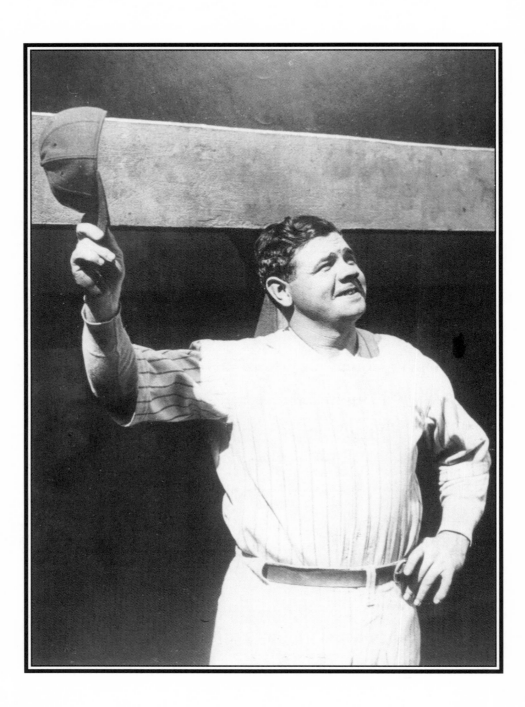

To the memory of
George Herman "Babe" Ruth; to the children
of America whom he loved; and to my editor,
Mark Alvarez, for sharing
my vision.

---

*"What I am, what I have, what I am
going to leave behind me—all this I
owe to the game of baseball."*

— **Babe Ruth**

Preface

My connection to baseball began at birth. Although the career of Hall-of-Fame slugger Jimmie Foxx had ended before I came into this world, "Double X" and I had one thing in common: we both hailed from Sudlersville, Maryland (population 417) on Maryland's rural Eastern Shore. I was raised on the legend and lore of Foxx. My father never read to me. Instead, he told me stories of The Beast's home runs splintering upper deck seats in ballparks throughout America. As a child, I walked on the town ball field, knowing that Foxx had played there. It was a magical experience.

Today, I live in Baltimore. Each evening as I drive home from work through the city's streets, I gaze at the Kernan Hotel where the 19-year-old Babe Ruth joined a group of Baltimore Orioles heading south for spring training on a snowy day in 1914. Every time I go to a game at Oriole Park I walk through the neighborhood where he grew up and I am filled with awe knowing Babe traveled these same streets. He left Baltimore to become the greatest baseball player of all time, forever changing the game, and becoming the most popular hero in our nation's history.

As a school librarian I am privileged to work with children. I am thrilled to see the wonder and excitement in their eyes at the mention of Babe Ruth. A full century after his birth, the Babe continues to hold a special place in the hearts of children, just as he did at the height of his career over sixty years ago. No individual has appealed to children in the same way.

Although Babe's flaws are almost as famous as his accomplishments, his human failings haven't dimmed his luster. This is because he earned America's respect and affection not merely as baseball's greatest player, but as a man who genuinely loved children and took the time to show it.

Heroes do not fit preestablished molds, but their importance to children is beyond measure. I believe that kids possess the innate wisdom to understand that heroes are not perfect. Children—and adults, too—can admire their achievements and learn from their mistakes. When we find out more about the lives of these people, we often discover pain and disappointment, along with triumph and accomplishment. All of these things are normal in everyone's life—even the life of a hero.

Babe Ruth had a tough childhood. In later years he himself said, "I was a bum." All during his career he resisted authority as he had as a child, and this cost him his fondest dream: to manage the Yankees after he retired as a player. Young readers can thrill to their heroes' accomplishments while seeing the high price of human error.

I am delighted that today's children remain keenly interested in the Sultan of Swat. That would have meant a great deal to the Babe. This book is written to honor both him and the children of America.

Lois P. Nicholson, Baltimore, MD
November, 1994

INNING ONE

The "Called Shot"

1932

*"I swing big with everything I've got. I hit big
or I miss big. I like to live as big as I can."*

A strong wind was blowing out toward left field at Chicago's Wrigley Field on the afternoon of October 1, 1932. But Babe Ruth never needed any help from the breezes. He was baseball's greatest home run hitter and the most popular player of all time. However, he had been met by an unfriendly welcome when he arrived in Chicago on the train the night before. It took a police escort to get the Yankees safely through the jostling crowds to their hotel; one woman got close enough to spit at Ruth and his wife. His New York Yankees were in town for Game 3 of the World Series, having demolished the Cubs, 12-6 and 5-2, in New York.

More insults than base hits had hurtled through the air during those two games. This was not unusual. Name-calling and slurs were routine in those days. For instance, if a pitcher hit a batter with a pitch, players rarely charged the mound. The batter mocked the pitcher, yelling "Hey Pitch, if you left a bruise on me, I'll buy you supper." Or he retaliated by stealing second.

But the verbal barbs were especially sharp that day. One of Ruth's pals on the Yankees, an infielder named Mark Koenig, had been acquired by the Cubs late in the season, and his hitting had helped them win the pennant. But the Cubs had voted to give Koenig only a half share of their World Series money. The Yankees thought that was no way to treat their old teammate and they didn't hesitate to say so to reporters. On the field they called the Cubs "tightfisted" and "skin-flints" and "misers." When the Cubs were in the dugout, the Yankees hollered, "Hey, Mark, who are those cheapskates with you?"

The sharp-tongued Cubs gave it right back. Aiming their barbs at Ruth, now 34 and potbellied, they let fly with an unmerciful barrage of custom-made insults. They singled out his hulking frame and large features, reminding Babe that he was fat, old, and washed up. It seemed funny to hear the jeers about Ruth being finished. He had batted .341 and hit 41 home runs that year. But the Cubs hoped to distract the slugger. They called him gorilla, ape, monkey, and Tarzan, yelling jibes like "Hey, you big baboon."

Such barbs were nothing new to Babe. He had been hearing them since his days at St. Mary's Industrial School in Baltimore where the other kids jeered him about his thick lips and large frame. However, one thing had changed since Ruth's childhood. As a boy, he'd answered with his fists. Now he spoke with his 52-ounce bat.

Before the game the fans threw lemons at Babe, who laughed and threw them back into the seats. None of it bothered Ruth, who always enjoyed himself, whatever he was doing. He was having the time of his life. In batting practice he and the Yankees' other great slugger, first baseman Lou Gehrig, put on a show that would have silenced more fainthearted foes. Between them they drove 16 balls into the bleachers as the Cubs looked on. Ruth grinned his quarter-moon smile and yelled at them, "I'd play for half my salary if I could hit in this dump all the time."

As the Cubs ran onto the field to start the game, their reserves and pitchers were on the dugout steps firing insults at Ruth, who batted third in the Yankee lineup. Even the trainer got into it: "If I had you, I'd hitch you to a wagon, you potbelly."

The first man up was safe on an error and the next batter walked. As Ruth strode to the plate, pitcher Charlie Root scowled down at him and the Cubs' chorus of razz intensified. Ruth took a few steps toward Chicago's third base dugout, yelled something into the cackling uproar, and gestured toward the right field bleachers. Then he stepped into the batters box and hit the third pitch into the bleachers for a 3-run homer.

In the third inning, Gehrig hit a solo homer, but the Cubs came back to tie it, 4-4. The 50,000 fans went wild with glee when Ruth tried to make a shoestring catch in right field and missed, allowing the tying run to score. The Cubs, determined to give the mighty Yankees the beating of their lives, smelled victory.

Waiting for his turn to bat in the fifth, Ruth was hit with another lemon from the stands. As the hostile hoots and hollers grew louder, the grin on Babe's face grew wider. The scrappy kid from a rough Baltimore neighborhood thrived on jawing and he loved every minute of it (except, he said later, when the trainer got on him: "I didn't mind no ballplayers yelling at me, but the trainer cutting in—that made me sore").

He took his left-handed batting stance and Root threw a strike past him. The other Cub pitchers—Bush, Malone, and Grimes—came out of the dugout onto the top step and yammered all the louder. Babe gave it right back to the cocky Cubs, wagging his right index finger at them, as if to say that was only one strike.

Root threw two pitches out of the strike zone, then slipped another good one past the Babe for strike two. Unable to contain himself, Guy

Cubs pitcher Charlie Root always said that if Ruth had actually pointed at the bleachers, he would have knocked him down on the next pitch.

Bush leaped out of the dugout onto the grass in anticipation. The great Bambino was about to strike out. But Babe had the confidence of a true champion. This time Ruth waved two fingers at them and hollered at Bush, "Hey Lop Ears. It only takes one to hit it." But the razzing was so loud that only the catcher heard Babe's warning.

From the mound, Root got into the verbal free-for-all. Ruth turned to face him and hollered back, "I'm going to knock the next pitch right down your . . . throat."

Babe, for all his fun-loving and showmanship, was a very smart ballplayer. He had been the league's best left-handed pitcher before moving to the outfield to have his bat in the lineup every day. Despite the raucous sideshow going on around him and his starring role in it, he was thinking right along with the pitcher: "Root threw fastballs by me for strikes, and he thinks I'll be looking for another one so he'll throw me a curve."

Root threw him a curve, low and outside, and Ruth, timing it perfectly, made contact with the ball. Babe drove it farther up into the center field bleachers than anybody had ever hit one. Not only could he jaw, he backed up his words like no one else who had every played the game.

Yankee shortstop Joe Sewell remembered Babe's shot. "That ball just went straight out and through a tree outside the ball park in center field. The tree was loaded with youngsters up there watching the game, and as the ball went through the tree all those kids evaporated. They had all gone after the ball."

Like a sultan, Babe trotted around the bases, feeling on top of the world. He thumbed his nose at the subdued Cubs as he rounded third. A barrage of cabbages, oranges, and apples rained down on him, but Babe didn't care. He reached home plate and was greeted by hugs from his gleeful teammates in pinstripes. Just a moment earlier, the Cubs had mocked Babe's ability. Now they stood in stunned silence.

The excitement was so electrifying that hardly anybody noticed Lou Gehrig step in and hit the first pitch into the right field bleachers. The Yankees won, 7 to 5, and continued their winning ways by polishing off Bush and the Cubs the next day, 13 to 6, to sweep the Series.

Soon after the Series ended, newspaper reports began claiming that Ruth had pointed to the center field bleachers before the final pitch— predicting his home run in front of a ballpark full of hostile fans. First one, then another writer picked up the idea. Like all good stories, this one was embellished with each telling. The writers were unable to resist making a good story even better, until it eventually became the Legend of the Called Shot.

The more people read about it, the more they became convinced that it had really happened. Many disciples of baseball wanted to believe it was true. Even people who had been at the game later swore they had seen him do it. It was as if everyone needed a single story that would best illustrate George Herman Ruth's immortal stature.

The Babe went along with the exaggerated tale; when asked about it, he never stated that he pointed to the bleachers. He also did not deny it. Smiling his signature grin, Babe fully enjoyed the story just as he thoroughly enjoyed life itself. Most players on both teams were certain that Ruth had been pointing at the Cubs dugout and jawing at them, and photographs of the action backed them up. But, as one player said, "It's a good story, so why not leave it that way."

Babe Ruth's first home run in the "called shot" game.

Whether or not it really happened, one fact endures. Then or now, no one except Babe Ruth was considered capable of such a daring display of bravado. It would be foolish for any player, even Ruth, to be so bold a braggart, to make so rash a prediction before 50,000 fans and risk the embarrassment of failing. But the fact that nobody, once they were told it had happened, doubted it for a second or put it past the Babe, is the strongest evidence of the unique position he held in the hearts of people all over the world. Even if he had struck out after "calling his shot" it would not have bothered the Babe, who declared, "I swing big, with everything I've got. I hit big or I miss big. I like to live as big as I can."

The Babe as a babe.

INNING TWO

A Baltimore Boy

1895-1912

"I was a bum."

altimore was a bustling port when George Herman Ruth, Jr. was born there on February 6, 1895. Ships from around the globe slowly sailed up the Chesapeake Bay to dock along the busy harbor as they continue to do today. Nearby, the city's teeming streets were lined with narrow brick rowhouses whose white marble front steps hugged the sidewalks. The backyards were much too small for even a game of catch.

In this setting, a stocky dark-haired young man, George Herman Ruth, the son of a saloonkeeper and grocer, had met and married a petite young woman, Katherine Schamberger, the daughter of German immigrants. Kate and George lived with his parents above the Ruths' noisy saloon and grocery on Frederick Avenue.

When Kate became pregnant with their first child, she chose to return to the home of her parents, Mr. and Mrs. Pius Schamberger, at 216 Emory Street for the birth. This house is now the Babe Ruth

Museum. The Schamberger residence, only 12 feet wide, was part of a 4-unit section of brick rowhouses lining the busy street where neighbors chatted to one another from their front stoops as the children played on the sidewalks. Inside, the narrow dwelling included a living room, a kitchen in the rear with a fireplace for cooking, and a winding staircase leading to two small upstairs bedrooms.

With the help of a local midwife, Minnie Graf, the Ruths' first child was born in the front bedroom. The boy was called Little George and his father Big George. Soon Kate and the infant returned to the Ruths' home on Frederick Avenue. Eventually, the young couple and their son settled in their own house on West Camden Street where Big George continued the family tradition, operating a saloon. The family lived upstairs in cramped quarters, with little space for a young boy to play.

George Herman Ruth, who grew up to be the Babe, was born in this brick rowhouse in Baltimore. The building is now the Babe Ruth Museum, within easy walking distance of Oriole Park at Camden Yards.

Located in South Baltimore, the rough neighborhood was close to the Baltimore and Ohio Railroad's main yard, the docks, and the city's pulsing downtown area. The streets and alleys were filled with railroad men, factory employees, dock workers, and teamsters at all hours of the day and night. Horsedrawn wagons hauled goods throughout the city. Clanging streetcars ran on lines woven into the cobblestone streets paved with ballast stones from cargo ships that sailed into the docks.

Big George tried his hand at a number of businesses, including selling lightning rods for buildings. But what he liked best was being a barkeep and, over the years, he operated six different saloons within the same community. The Ruths moved six times: with each move, the family occupied the rooms above the bar.

Ruth's West Camden Street bar was a dark, smoke-filled room, patronized by the neighborhood workers who passed the time telling stories laced with loud profanity. As these rough men laughed heartily, they swatted flies that entered through the open door during the summer months. A pressed tin ceiling overlooked the bar, which featured a long copper spit box where the patrons spat their brown tobacco juice. The men rested their weary feet on a brass rail beneath the bar before finally going home to prepare for the next day's labor.

Kate toiled by her husband's side from morning to late at night, Monday through Saturday. Little George later remembered that his parents often worked 20-hour days. Until her death at age 37, Kate Ruth knew much sorrow. She gave birth to seven more babies, including two sets of twins. Tragically, George and his sister, Mary Margaret, born in 1900, where the only children to survive infancy. One of Kate's greatest joys came when her sister, Mary, visited. The two women chatted eagerly in German so the children could not understand their conversations. When Kate reprimanded Little George and his sister, she boxed their ears. If she happened to use the left hand with her wedding ring, the blow carried an additional wallop.

Little George seemed to thrive on Kate's German cooking, growing like a cornfield in August. He inherited his father's large features, dark hair, and tall, stocky build. He looked older than his age, towering over his younger sister who was small like her mother. Soon, George was hanging around the saloon, snatching cigarettes from customers when their backs were turned and emptying the beer and whiskey glasses left on the bar.

Busy with their work, the Ruths had little time to entertain their children who longed to play outside with their friends. Feeling like caged creatures inside the narrow house, George and Mary, or Mamie as he called her, often gazed out their upstairs window facing the massive red brick B & O Warehouse which now overlooks Oriole Park at Camden Yards, home of the Baltimore Orioles. They watched as trucks backed up to the warehouse's huge doors, unloading or taking on cargo.

Factories surrounded the Camden Street neighborhood forming a high brick canyon. There were no recreation centers, playgrounds, or vacant lots. Children played on the sidewalks or in the streets, carefully sidestepping the plentiful horse manure dotting the gray cobblestones. The girls preferred hopscotch or jumprope, while the boys played stick ball, a rubber ball and a crude stick taking the place of a hardball and bat. George escaped the confinement of the rowhouse by gradually spending more and more time roaming the streets with his companions who, as his sister recalled, "were the lowest kind." Mr. and Mrs. Ruth seldom knew the whereabouts of their young son. Like a sponge, George absorbed the character of the neighborhood, becoming rough and scrappy. "I learned to fear and hate the coppers and to throw apples and eggs at the truckdrivers . . . I was a bum when I was a kid," he later admitted.

When George entered public school, he felt hopelessly trapped inside all day. Although he left the house each morning bound for classes, George often hooked school, hiding in the murky alleys bordering the docks. "The truant officer spent more time at our house than his own," remembered Mamie. In the shadows of the looming warehouses, George received daily lessons in the seamy side of city life.

When his parents learned that George was playing hooky, they ordered Mamie to watch her brother enter the school each morning. However, Mamie was no match for George, who merely walked in one door and out another, then headed for the haven of the alleys once again, sporting a big grin on his broad, mischievous face. Stubborn and impulsive, he simply refused to obey his parents and the school officials. It seemed that everyone was conspiring to contain him, but George was determined to show the world that he was his own boss. In his autobiography Ruth said, "I honestly don't remember being aware of the difference between right and wrong."

Despite his bad habits, George was very likeable. Usually easygoing, there was something about his friendly nature that appealed to everyone. However, like his father, at times he possessed a vicious temper. Big George attempted to punish his son by beating him, but the boy responded by cursing his father before running out the door. At other times, he merely laughed heartily as Big George's huge hand found its stubborn mark. The Ruths knew that their son needed a firm hand. They found the solution in St. Mary's Industrial School.

George was seven when he first walked through the gates of St. Mary's on June 13, 1902. Although it was Friday the 13th, it was one of the luckiest days of his life. Located in southwest Baltimore, St. Mary's was a Catholic training school for delinquent boys. It also provided

During the Babe's childhood, his father, far right, owned several saloons. Here, a grown Babe, center, is helping tend bar.

shelter for orphans and sons of poor or troubled families who could not properly care for them. The school's 800 residents were supervised by Xaverian Brothers, men who chose to serve the church, often as teachers. The students, ranging in age from seven to 21, lived in four sparsely furnished dormitories, each housing 200 cots. They received clothing, food, shelter, schooling, and religious instruction. George's parents paid $15 a month, a large sum of money at the time, for their son to live at St. Mary's, but they viewed it as a wise investment in George's future.

Classroom at St. Mary's.

The school provided the boys with much-needed discipline, but the residents were permitted to leave for special occasions, and the grounds were not fenced in. For the first time in their young lives, the students experienced structure and a strict schedule. Rules were clear and enforced by punishments. They began their days at 6:00 A.M., bathed, dressed, ate breakfast, and attended Mass before beginning classes at 7:30. Lunch was the only break from a full day spent in classrooms and workshops until the late afternoon when the students enjoyed an hour of recreation before supper.

The highlight of each day was the treasured "rec" period, held outside in a huge area known as The Yard. The younger boys played in the Little Yard while the older students occupied the Big Yard. From March into the fall, they played baseball, turning to other sports in winter. One of George's favorite games was pokem. One player with a bat stood in front of a wall while the other player pitched to him. The batter could remain up until the pitcher struck him out and the boys then traded positions.

After supper, a candy shop opened for one hour. The boys earned credits in the workshops for the purchase of candy and cakes, prized treats to brighten the school's bland menus. Lights were out by 8:00 and the next day was a carbon copy of the day before. Sundays provided a welcome change of pace when family members could visit during the afternoon.

On Kate Ruth's only day off from the saloon, she and Mamie took the streetcar to visit George. Mamie recalled that she and her mother made the trek, "rain or shine, snow or blow." They carried a basket brimming with fruits, candies, and cookies which he readily shared with the many boys who had no visitors.

George was left-handed, but in those days being a "lefty" was considered a handicap. It was common for teachers to tie children's left hands behind their backs so that they could not write with the "wrong" hand. Despite these conditions, George developed unusually graceful handwriting using his right hand. But other than his fine penmanship, he never cared much about school work.

Instead, George liked to work with his hands. He excelled in vocational training, learning carpentry and rolling cigars before he finally settled in the tailor shop where the boys made shirts. A student named Lawton Stenersen worked with George. "We got six cents a shirt from the Oppenheim Shirt Company," he recalled. George became a joiner, sewing on collars. He took great pride in his work. In fact, years later, when he could afford the very finest shirts, he still preferred turning the collars himself on his mother-in-law's sewing machine.

Brother Mathias was in charge of discipline. He ruled the school with an iron hand, aided by his imposing 6-foot-6-inch, 250-pound frame. The boys called him the Boss and, without question, he was. In his calm manner, he firmly and fairly guided the students, endearing himself to them while earning their complete respect. Once, when a massive brawl broke out in the yard, Brother Mathias merely watched from an elevated spot in full view of all the students. Standing like a statue, with his arms folded, he never spoke a word. The boys, seeing the Boss, quickly ended their fisticuffs.

George was well liked and made friends easily. When a new boy, Jerry DeLay, entered the school, George attempted to welcome him by inviting him to play catch. DeLay, built like a linebacker, responded by punching Ruth. The two boys were suddenly embroiled in a fight. Other students quickly jumped onto the heap of flailing bodies. Brother Mathias appeared out of the blue, reached into the pile, and extracted DeLay from the group.

As the others stood and watched in wonder, he carried away the boy tucked under his arm like a sack of feathers. But George and DeLay quickly became friends. The Babe was never one to hold a grudge.

George had sorely tested the authority of his parents, but he loved and respected Brother Mathias, who saw in George a large, friendly kid with a great deal of athletic potential. He understood that the boy's talents and energies needed to be channeled in a positive direction. Baseball was the answer. At every opportunity he demonstrated the fundamental skills of the game to his eager student. As George looked on, Brother Mathias tossed the ball in the air and hit powerful fungos by swinging the bat with one hand. Awestruck, George watched his towering instructor and dreamed of being that kind of slugger. "I think I was born as a hitter the first day I ever saw him hit a baseball," Ruth later observed.

George proved to be a natural with the bat, but his fielding skills were lacking. Brother Mathias worked with him to develop his talents as a catcher. "I could hit the first time I picked up a bat," Ruth said, "but Brother Mathias made me a fielder."

George remained at the school for 10 years. He returned home to live now and then, but trouble always seemed to find him, and he ended up back at St. Mary's. George spent two years away from the school following his mother's death in 1910, but he returned when he was 16.

He had grown to become a tall young man. A thicket of dark hair cropped close to his large head crowned a slim frame featuring long arms and legs. But inside he remained a street kid. Once when the frigid winter wind blasted across the yard, Brother Paul saw that he wasn't wearing a coat and expressed concern. "Don't you think you should have a coat on?"

George shot back, "Not me, Brother, I'm tough."

Despite his roots in a rough neighborhood and his coarse appearance, George developed into a person known for his kindness to others at St. Mary's. The brothers believed that the students should spend a full hour outside in the fresh air whatever the weather. On the snow-covered playing fields many of the younger boys would run to George, who rubbed their small hands as he blew on their aching fingers.

When George found a younger boy crying because he had broken a window in the laundry, he ordered, "Go on, get out of here. Take it on the lam." George then accepted the blame for the broken window.

Throughout his life, money meant little to Ruth. He gave away his earnings from the workshop at St. Mary's so kids who had no friends or relatives could buy candy. Everyone looked up to the popular, gangly teenager with a heart of gold. Lawton Stenersen later described George's role at St. Mary's, "He made life a little more livable when life seemed unbearable."

Brother Mathias believed in George, and George wanted to please the man who had shown such interest in him. Although he would come to know presidents and movie stars, he never forgot St. Mary's or Brother Mathias, whom he called "the greatest man I've ever known."

St. Mary's Industrial School for Boys, young George Ruth's home from the time he was seven until he signed with the Baltimore Orioles of the Eastern League.

INNING THREE

St. Mary's Ace Pitcher

1912-1914

"I never lost my taste for hitting and don't ever expect to."

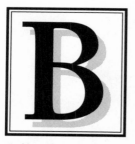

aseball in the spring of 1912 was a thriving sport throughout America. Against a backdrop of new green grass and budding trees, players across the country breathed fresh air filled with the hope that every new baseball season brings. In Baltimore, hundreds of amateur and semipro teams played regularly scheduled games. St. Mary's fielded 40 different teams, organized by age levels. Under Brother Mathias's watchful eye, Brother Albin, a young man in his 20s, coached baseball at St. Mary's and played first base. Brother Albin organized the older and more talented students in a formal league, calling the teams the Cubs, Giants, Red Sox, and White Sox.

When George first arrived at St. Mary's, he had only played stickball using crude equipment, but he quickly excelled in baseball. George showed exceptional skill behind the plate. His friend at St. Mary's, Louis Leisman, remembered hearing George Ruth's name for the first time as a rumor spread throughout the school. The dormitories were structured according to the students' ages. Number 2 was for boys 15 and older and Number 3 for boys under 15.

"What's going on?" asked Louis.

"Number 2 dormitory is going to play Number 3, and George Ruth is going to catch for Number 3."

A left-handed catcher then, as today, was rare. George caught wearing the mitt on his left hand, his throwing hand. After catching a ball, he jabbed the mitt beneath his right arm, grabbed the ball with his left hand, and rifled it with all his might. George was playing for St. Mary's championship team—the Red Sox—in 1912, when a photograph

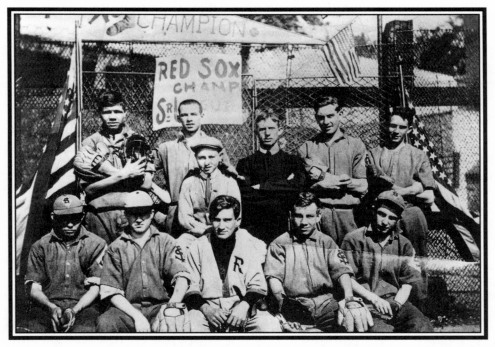

The Babe, upper left, used a right-hander's catcher's mitt even though he was left-handed.

shows him sporting the mitt on his left hand. But in another photo he appears wearing the mitt on his right hand, indicating that he probably alternated.

Mount St. Joseph's baseball coach, Brother Gilbert, remembered the young catcher's impressive arm. "He was catching for one of the teams in a league they had at St. Mary's, and if you ever wanted to see a bone out of joint or one of nature's misfits, you should have seen him, a left-handed catcher squatting behind the plate. All he had was a mask and a glove, which he wore on his left hand," Brother Gilbert said. "And how he could throw! The ball was three feet off the ground going through the box and three feet off the ground when it got to second base."

Although George first made a name for himself as a catcher, he also tried his strong arm on the mound. According to one story, he replaced a starting pitcher who was benched, but George admitted that Brother Mathias placed him on the rubber for another reason. The Red Sox were being soundly walloped by another team when Brother Mathias noticed George chuckling at his own pitcher. He inquired about the source of George's amusement.

George confessed that he thought his team's pitching was a joke. "All right, George," responded Brother Mathias, "You pitch."

Behind his catcher's mask, the broad grin dropped like a dying quail. "Me?" he asked. "I don't know how to pitch."

"Oh, you must know a lot about it," Mathias said confidently. "You know enough to know that your friend here isn't any good. Go ahead out there and show us how it's done."

To everyone's surprise, especially his own, George did well on the mound. "As soon as I got out there I felt a strange relationship with the pitcher's mound," he later said. "It was as if I'd been born out there. Pitching just felt like the most natural thing in the world. Striking out batters was easy."

Babe considered Brother Mathias the "greatest man I've ever known."

But what he really did best was hit. His homers sailed out of the yard, capturing everyone's attention and sending notice that George was no slouch with the lumber.

Brother Gilbert recognized George's pitching and hitting talents. "I knew that with an arm like that he could be made into a pitcher. And then I saw him go to bat...There he stood, just as you saw him standing at the plate when he was at the peak of his career. There was determination in his attitude—he had the will to do . . . And he looked better striking out than he did hitting home runs."

The next season, 1913, marked George's final year at St. Mary's. As a farewell message, he hit a home run in almost every game. He was undefeated whenever he pitched. For the first time, his name appeared on a Baltimore sports page. On June 8, 1913 the Baltimore *American* reported that the St. Mary's Stars downed the White Sox, 10-3, with Button on the mound and Ruth catching.

That summer, George pitched for St. Mary's but he was granted permission to leave the school on weekends to play with amateur and semipro teams. In August a newspaper account of one game reported, "Ruth, the Bayonne fencebuster, was there with the willow."

Early in his big league career he summed up his St. Mary's record. "I wasn't a pitcher in those days until I was pretty nearly through. My main job was catching, though I also played first base and the outfield. I used to hit .450 and .500. I kept track one season and found that I made over 60 home runs. The last two years I pitched and got along pretty well, but I never lost my taste for hitting and don't ever expect to."

George's reputation as a pitcher with a hot bat was spreading. Although no one is certain exactly how word of his talent reached the Baltimore Orioles of the Eastern League [the modern Orioles entered the American League in 1954], one story involved a game between St. Mary's and Mount St. Joseph's College. Joe Engel, a pitcher for the

Washington Senators, was in the stands that day as George took the mound.

Not only was Engel impressed with George's delivery, he noticed the 18-year-old hurler's stylish haircut. The bartenders and fashionable young men from George's Camden Street neighborhood wore their hair cropped short on the sides and "roached" or waved down over their foreheads. A schoolboy making a fashion statement stood out in Engel's memory, but more important, George threw smoke. "He really could wheel that ball in there," recalled Engel, "and remember, I was used to seeing Walter Johnson throw. [Johnson, who won over 400 games for the Senators, is often considered baseball's fastest pitcher.] This kid was a great natural pitcher. He had everything. He must have struck out 18 or 20 men in that game." The school bands performed after the game and Engel spotted George pounding the bass drum for St. Mary's.

Returning to Washington that evening, Engel ran into Jack Dunn, the owner of the Orioles. When Engel explained where he had been, Dunn asked him if anyone had caught his eye. From the backwoods to the big city, scouts were constantly bird-dogging or sniffing out new talent.

"Yeah. There was some orphan asylum from Baltimore playing and they had a young left-handed kid pitching for them who's got real stuff," responded Engel. With a slow grin spreading across his face, he added, "He can also beat hell out of a bass drum."

Taking a pencil and paper from his pocket, Dunn asked, "You don't happen to remember his name, do you?"

"I think they called him Ruth," said Engel.

In 1913, Mount St. Joe's boasted a star pitcher, Bill Morrisette. The Xaverian Brothers, who ran both St. Mary's and St. Joe's, bragged to one another about their ace hurlers. The Brothers scheduled a showdown between Ruth and Morrisette. When Jack Dunn learned about the pitching duel between Morrisette and Ruth, he was eager to see the game.

As the big contest approached, St. Mary's pulsed with excitement. The boys felt the "rich kids and snobs" from St. Joe's looked down on them, but with George on the mound, they hoped to taste the sweetness of kicking the college boys in their wealthy pants. St. Mary's would host the game on their home field. Each day, after Mass, classes, and work in the shops, the boys swept, scrubbed, and polished their turf. At night, dreams of victory filled the dormitories like 800 silent movies.

But the sweet dreams suddenly turned into despair. The boys awoke one morning several days before the game to learn that George had run away during the night, climbing through a dormitory window and disappearing. A Baltimore boy, Everett Abbott, later recalled Babe bragging about running away whenever he felt like it. But the kids at St. Mary's couldn't understand how he could let them down at such a critical time.

For the next three days, school officials combed the city's docks and alleys searching for their star pitcher. Classes were canceled as the Brothers met to discuss the crisis. The students huddled together, sharing the latest rumors, their vigil stretching into each evening as they watched members of the search party return emptyhanded. Then word spread over the campus like a flash flood of hope: George was back. No one knew where he had gone or why, and the Brothers told the boys to ask no questions. George had returned. Nothing else mattered.

Jack Dunn joined the huge crowd that lined St. Mary's field on the day of the game. Bunting and flags waved in the warm summer breeze. The air was charged with excitement as George threw the first pitch. Nine innings later he had devastated Morrisette and St. Joe's in a 6-0 shutout, striking out 22 batters. It was St. Mary's finest hour.

On February 14, 1914, two weeks before the Baltimore Orioles

The Babe on one of his later visits to St. Mary's.

would leave for spring training, Dunn returned to St. Mary's. George had just celebrated his 19th birthday and the playing field was covered with snow.

Brother Paul, St. Mary's superintendent, was George's legal guardian until he reached the age of 21. The Orioles needed his permission to sign Ruth to a professional contract paying $600 for the season. Jack Dunn was highly respected in Baltimore and Brother Paul decided to release George in Dunn's custody.

George spent two more weeks at St. Mary's. On Friday, February 27 the following entry was made in St. Mary's ledger: "He is going to join the Balt. Baseball team."

The wayward seven-year-old boy who had entered St. Mary's gates was now a 19-year-old man, standing 6 feet 2 inches tall and weighing 160 pounds. George said goodbye to his friends and shook hands with the Brothers. Finally, he turned to the man who had been the most influential person in his life, the man who had believed in him and had introduced him to baseball, Brother Mathias.

As Ruth looked into the Brother's eyes, he knew how much he owed this great man. Brother Mathias, still four inches taller than George, took the young man's large hand in his own. Clasping it firmly, he spoke quietly and confidently as always. "You'll make it, George," he predicted.

INNING FOUR

From Baltimore to the Bigs

1914

*"I hit it as I hit all the others, by taking a good gander
at the pitch, twisting my body into a backswing and
then hitting it as hard as I could swing."*

he biting winter air filled Ruth's lungs as he stepped from the streetcar on Friday, February 27, 1914. The frigid temperatures reminded him that in three days he would be far away from Baltimore's chill. He made his way through the familiar neighborhood to his father's Conway Street saloon. On Monday afternoon, the 19-year-old was to meet a group of Jack Dunn's Baltimore Orioles at the Kernan Hotel. Ruth had never traveled more than 50 miles from home. By Monday night, he and the other players would be bound for the Orioles spring training camp in Fayetteville, North Carolina.

When Ruth awoke on Sunday in the bedroom above his father's bar, a cold wind was howling. Throughout the day, the thermometer plunged and snow began to blanket the quiet streets. By evening, the entire northeast was crippled by a major blizzard that raged into Monday morning. Some of Dunn's players were unable to reach the hotel that afternoon, but no mere blizzard was going to stop Ruth. He had never ridden on a train in his life, and he was determined to be at Union Station with the others.

On Monday evening, the train carrying Ruth and his fellow Orioles pulled out of Baltimore, headed for the warmth of the south. Accompanying Ruth was Bill Morrisette, the pitcher for St. Joe's, whom Dunn had also signed. When the veteran players learned that Ruth had never traveled by train, they decided to have some fun with him. A small hammock for clothes hung above each Pullman berth. But the older players told Ruth that it was for pitchers to rest their pitching arms. The gullible rookie dutifully slept with his left arm in the hammock. The next morning, his arm was painfully stiff as he and the other players walked to the Lafayette Hotel.

Ruth and his teammates were disappointed that the temperature in Fayetteville was unusually cold, but by afternoon the sun warmed the city's Fair Grounds where the Orioles trained. Like young colts romping in a spring pasture, the prospects, mostly pitchers, lobbed balls to

"Dunn's Babe," fifth from left, front row, looks at ease with his Baltimore teammates in 1914.

one another. As they threw, they were filled with the sweet realization that an entire season stretched endlessly before them, a dream hitched to a rainbow.

Over the next few days, the remaining Orioles arrived in camp and training was soon in full swing. During that era, baseball writers roomed with players and even joined them for practice games. Rodger Pippen of the Baltimore *News-Post* was Ruth's first roommate in professional baseball.

On Saturday, March 7 Ruth played his first game as a professional ballplayer. Hundreds of fans, hungry for baseball after a long winter, lined the Fair Grounds' diamond. The team paired off into two squads, the Sparrows and the Buzzards, for a scrub game. The left-handed Ruth played shortstop for the Buzzards whose outfield included writer Rodger Pippen. With one man on in the second inning, Ruth stepped up to the plate. Pippen wrote the following account of what happened next. "The next batter made a hit that will live in the memory of all who saw it. The clouter was George Ruth, the southpaw from St. Mary's school. The ball carried so far to right field that he walked around the bases." As Ruth crossed the plate, Morrisette, who was playing outfield for the Sparrows, was just plucking the ball from the cornfield beyond right-center.

A sign still marks the spot in Fayetteville where Ruth hit his first professional home run. Babe never forgot it. "I hit it as I hit all the others, by taking a good gander at the pitch, twisting my body into a backswing and then hitting it as hard as I could swing."

Baltimore awoke on March 8, 1914 to a lazy Sunday morning. Many citizens retrieved editions of the Sunday papers from their white marble stoops. Turning to the sports section, readers were greeted with headlines about a Baltimore boy who had left town just six days earlier. "HOMER BY RUTH FEATURE OF GAME," declared the Baltimore *Sun*. The *American* boasted, "RUTH MAKES MIGHTY CLOUT."

Not only had Ruth routed the Sparrows with his bat, he took the mound for the final two innings, hurling fastballs like a seasoned pro. Ben Egan, the team's big catcher and Dunn's field captain, immediately liked Ruth. The veteran Egan took the young Ruth under his wing, but many years later the catcher confessed, "He knew how to pitch the first day I saw him. I didn't have to tell him anything. He knew how to hold runners on base, and he knew how to work on the hitters."

When Jack Dunn listed the players he would keep for the regular season, Ruth's name appeared. Delighted with the Baltimore rookie, Dunn openly praised Ruth. "He has all the earmarks of a great ballplayer," said the Orioles owner. "He hits like a fiend and he seems to be at home in any position, even though he's left-handed. He's the most promising young ballplayer I've ever had." Dunn was right. It was as if Ruth had been born playing baseball.

He was a natural, but he hadn't perfected the finer points of the game. Veteran players could sniff out any weakness. Nothing escaped their hawkish eyes. To gain the slightest edge, they studied a player's every move. The opposition quickly observed that Ruth curled his tongue at the corner of his mouth each time he threw a curve. Such habits were called "telegraphing" or signaling a pitch. Knowing what was coming, hitters hammered the rookie until he learned to keep his tongue in check.

Although Ruth looked like an experienced player, in other areas his behavior was childlike. Living at St. Mary's since he was seven, Ruth had never known life outside the institution or the streets of South Baltimore. Suddenly, he was in a new town, with the freedom to come and go as he wanted. He continued his habit of awaking each morning at 6:00, eager to explore the world with boyish curiosity. In the morning's first light, he headed for the train station. Intrigued by the power of the massive engines, he delighted in watching the huge locomotives racing by before he hurried back to the hotel for breakfast.

Meals at St. Mary's had been spartan. With 800 boys to feed, portions had been small and Ruth never seemed to get his fill. Now he marveled at the fact that he could order anything and the Orioles paid the tab. To celebrate, the slender Ruth shoveled food in his mouth as if each meal might be his last. His teammates watched in wide-eyed wonder. They had never seen a human consume such vast quantities of grub at one sitting. His roommate, Pippen, declared, "If I hadn't seen it, I wouldn't have believed it."

Nothing escaped Ruth's notice. When Jack Dunn loaned the young prospect five dollars for spending money, Ruth bribed the hotel's elevator man to allow him to operate the elevator. The rookie rode from the ground floor to the top, stopping at every floor, opening the doors, and peeking around before resuming the game like a kid with a new toy on Christmas.

Ruth also continued to display a talent for finding trouble. Growing up, he had longed for a bicycle, but his family could not afford such a luxury. He borrowed a two-wheeler in Fayetteville and quickly learned to ride. He sped around a corner one day, just as Jack Dunn walked around the bend into Ruth's path. Dunn dodged the bike and its rider, who crashed into the back of a wagon. Ruth landed with a thud, the bike wrapped around him. "If you want to go back to the home, kid," barked Dunn, "just keep riding those bicycles."

Despite his recklessness, Ruth's teammates liked the kid's good-natured approach to life. Many of the players were much older, and they were amused by Ruth's childlike enthusiasm. Soon the veterans dubbed him "Dunn's Babe." Three weeks after arriving in Fayetteville, George Herman Ruth became known as Babe Ruth to everyone. The name stuck.

The Babe's innocence extended onto the playing field. Ruth did not know the famous players and he feared no one. Likewise, the stars did not yet know Babe, but he soon made a lasting impression on the game's greatest players. "We had never heard of this kid," recalled Casey Stengel of the Brooklyn Dodgers. "But they told me to play him way out in right field. I did and he hit one over my head. The next time he came up to bat I played out so far they could see only my cap sticking out from the tall grass. He hit another one over my head, farther than any human was supposed to hit a ball."

The Baltimore club returned to their home field, Oriole Park at 29th and Greenmount, for regular season play. All games were played during the day, and ballparks were constructed so that the batter would not have to look into the late afternoon sun. The throwing arm of a left-handed pitcher on the mound usually faced the south. These pitchers became known as south-paws. Ruth immediately became his hometown's favorite southpaw hurler.

In the rookie's first start for the Birds, he beat Buffalo, 6 to 0. He followed that feat with a pinch-hit triple the next day. Soon the fans flocked by streetcar or on foot to see the kid from West Camden Street. (Few cars existed and there were no parking spaces.) On the days Ruth took the mound, the wooden stands overflowed with well-dressed men and women. In those days, people did not own leisure clothes. They dressed up for

After Babe crashed his bike, Dunn threatened to send him back to St. Mary's.

all occasions including church, picnics, and America's favorite pastime, baseball games. Ruth and his teammates won their first 13 games. But despite their winning ways, it was clear that Babe was the attraction. On the days when he did not pitch, as few as 150 fans were in attendance. The Federal League Terrapins, a major league team, were drawing huge crowds in their new facility across the street, Terrapin Park.

Formed in 1914 as a third major league, the Feds hoped to share the success of the existing National and American Leagues by luring some of their best players with large salaries. (When the Federal League folded in 1916, the Orioles moved into the new Terrapin Park, renamed it Oriole Park, and tore down the park where Ruth had pitched. The former Terrapin Park burned in 1944.)

Once the 1914 season began, Ruth received $50 twice a month. He had never dreamed of earning so much. With his very first pay, he went out and bought what he had always longed for: a bicycle. Despite his new prominence, he did not forget about his friends, asking Dunn for six game passes for boys from St. Mary's. Dunn quickly raised Ruth's salary to $1,800 a year, not only as a reward for his performance, but also in the hope of keeping his prized rookie from jumping to the Federal League.

But it was soon obvious that no matter how well the minor-league Orioles played, they could not compete with the big league Terrapins. They were losing money. Jack Dunn was a good businessman, but he had large loans to repay. He had gone into debt to sign his veteran players to handsome three-year contracts to keep them from going with the Feds. Dunn had to raise some quick cash. Although he hated to lose his top players, their cash value made a sale very tempting.

Dunn began unloading his best players. On July 10 Ben Egan, Ruth and star pitcher Ernie Shore were sold to the Boston Red Sox. The next day, Ruth and his teammates got on a train headed for Beantown and the major leagues.

The Babe as a young Red Sox phenom in 1915. He was rough, tough, and very, very good.

INNING FIVE

The Busher Comes to Boston

1914-1918

*"Because I liked to hit and took my turn in batting
practice with the regulars, I found all my bats sawed
in half when I came to my locker the next day."*

uth, Egan and Shore arrived at Boston's Back Bay
Station on Saturday morning, July 11, 1914.
They ate breakfast in Lander's coffee shop, where
Ruth met a pretty 16-year-old waitress, Helen
Woodford. Before he had downed his final cup of
coffee, Ruth had fallen for the young woman. In
the following weeks, he dined there often. The
three players went to Fenway Park where they met manager Bill
Carrigan. The Red Sox were in sixth place with a record of 40 wins and
38 losses. The manager wasted no time. He started Ruth against
Cleveland that afternoon.

During his first inning in the major leagues, Ruth faced Shoeless
Joe Jackson. Jackson singled, but Ruth ended the inning by picking
him off first base. Although Ruth was lifted after seven innings, the Sox
held on to win, 4 to 3. Just five months after leaving St. Mary's School,
the Babe had his first major league win. But when he lost to Detroit in

43

his next outing, Carrigan benched him. Although the Babe showed he could play, many of the older Red Sox thought he was too brash and boastful. He tended to hot dog, showing off and taking batting practice with the veterans, which rookies in those days did not do.

Then as today, many of the lower-level minor leagues were located in remote areas of the country. They were known as the "bush" leagues and the players were known as "bushers."

"The Red Sox wanted no part of me as a busher," Ruth recalled. "Because I liked to hit and took my turn in batting practice with the regulars, I found all my bats sawed in half when I came to my locker the next day."

Showboating had no place in baseball during those years. There was a strict, unwritten code of conduct. If a player hit a home run, he rounded the bases quickly with his head down. The slugger received a handshake from the batter in the on-deck circle. There were no high-fives. Boasting in any way invited a knock-down pitch the next time the braggart stepped up to the plate. It was signaled by the catcher who flicked his thumb upward against his curved index-finger, indicating the boaster was "going down."

There were standards for the way players wore their uniforms. Pantlegs were worn high; it was considered sloppy to allow them to droop below the knee. And if a player had worn jewelry on the field, he would have been laughed right out of the game.

Following his second loss Ruth was sent to the Sox minor league team in Providence, Rhode Island. Returning to Boston in September, he got his first hit in the majors on October 2, a double off the Yankees' King Cole. From July 11 to the end of the season, the Red Sox were 51-24, and finished second to Connie Mack's Philadelphia Athletics. The Babe was 24-10 for Baltimore, Providence, and Boston.

Two weeks after the close of the season, Ruth and Helen returned to Baltimore where they were quietly married. The newlyweds spent that winter helping Big George and his new wife tend Mr. Ruth's saloon. However, the Babe and his stepmother did not get along, and the young couple were relieved when spring training arrived in 1915.

Starting his second season with Boston, the southpaw was hot on the mound and at the plate. He slammed his first home run on May 6 in New York, but the news of his feat was buried under the headlines reporting that a German submarine had sunk the great ocean liner, the Lusitania. The scent of war blew in the wind, stirring the stars and stripes flying above the nation's ballparks. But Americans forgot about their problems when they went to the ballpark.

The Red Sox won the pennant and took the World Series from the Phillies in five games; Ruth did not get to pitch in the Series. He completed his first full year in the majors with an 18-8 record and was rec-

The 1915 Red Sox, the second of Boston's four championship squads during the 'teens, and the first World Series winners Babe ever played for. (Babe is in the third row, sixth from left.)

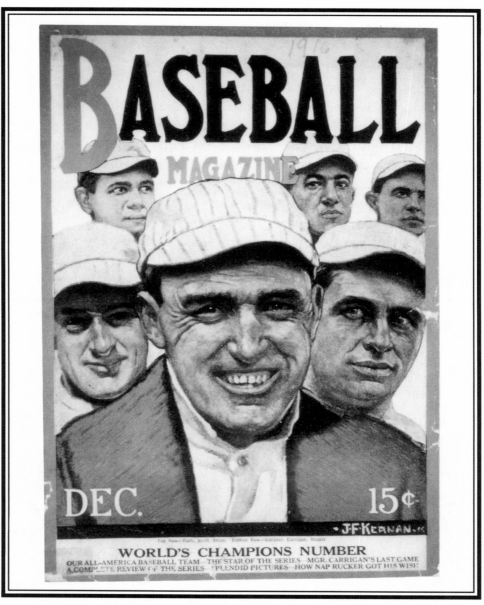

Manager Bill "Rough" Carrigan and the stars of his 1916 World Champion Boston Red Sox.

ognized as a pitcher with promise. However, pitching every four days severely limited Ruth's at bats. (His role as a hurler may have diminished his career home run total by 100.)

In 1916, Ruth's pitching remained impressive. When he won a five-hitter in New York a sportswriter wrote, "His name is Babe Ruth. He is built like a bale of cotton and pitches left-handed for the Boston Red Sox. All left-handers are peculiar and Babe is no exception, because he can also bat."

No one expected pitchers to be great hitters. Some players, like Ty Cobb, felt that Ruth's hitting skills were strengthened because he experimented at the plate. "No one cares much if a pitcher strikes out or looks bad at bat, so Ruth could take that big swing," explained Cobb. "If he missed, it didn't matter. And when he didn't miss, the ball went a long way. As time went on, he learned more and more about how to control that big swing and put the wood on the ball."

Not only was Babe enjoying success at the plate, he also liked the new lifestyle his $3,500 contract afforded. Just a few years earlier, the biggest treats in his life were the sweets his mother and Mamie brought to him at St. Mary's. Now he could have anything money could buy and lots of it. It was like a dream. He was being paid a great salary to do what he loved most in the world—play baseball. But the money flowed through his fingers like water through a sieve. Babe's pay evaporated during poker games. He often loaned money to teammates without asking to be repaid.

Manager Carrigan became increasingly concerned over Ruth's lack of financial discipline. He realized the Babe had no idea how to handle money. "He'd buy anything and everything," Carrigan remembered. "So, I would draw Babe's pay and give him a little every day to spend. That didn't last too long. At the end of the season I had to give him the rest of it. I calculated it wouldn't last too long, but that was the best I could do."

The Boston staff: Ernie Shore, Dutch Leonard, Rube Foster, Babe Ruth. Shore pitched his famous "perfect game" when he came in to relieve the Babe, who had been thrown out for arguing after walking the first batter he faced.

The Babe had never liked rules. It seemed that life was always trying to contain him. Confined in a rowhouse and an institution for most of his life, he finally had open spaces and a fat wallet. Yet people were still telling him what to do. For instance, Ruth resented the team's midnight curfew. The Babe paid little attention to the clock, but Carrigan kept a watchful eye on his wayward rookie, who liked the nightlife. The manager made sure Ruth's hotel room was next to his. Like Brother Mathias, Carrigan commanded Ruth's full respect. He also knew how to handle the Babe.

Carrigan was relieved when Ruth made a good friend. A young left-handed pitcher, Herb Pennock, joined the Red Sox in midseason. The quiet Pennock and Babe were as different as night and day, but the two southpaws struck up a lasting friendship. Pennock became a positive influence on his impulsive teammate.

Ruth pitched the Red Sox to their second straight pennant with 23 wins in 1916. Boston faced the Brooklyn Dodgers in the World Series. The Babe started the second game against the Dodgers under a threatening October sky at Fenway. After Ruth set down the first two Dodger batters, Hy Myers lined the ball to the right center field gap for an inside-the-park home run. But the 21-year-old Babe remained as cool as the fall weather. Although the contest went into extra innings, the Dodgers never scored again. Ruth remained on the mound, going 14 innings for the 2-1 win. It was the longest game in World Series history.

After the game, Ruth romped around the clubhouse like a boy, hugging his teammates and Carrigan. "I told you a year ago I could take care of those National League Bums," shouted Babe. "And you never gave me a chance."

Carrigan chuckled at Ruth's joy. "Forget it Babe," he laughed. "You made monkeys out of them today."

The Red Sox took the series in five games for the second straight year. Bill Carrigan, who was retiring after 12 years as a Boston player and manager, walked out onto the field after the final game, tipping his cap to the jubilant Boston fans. Ruth eventually played for seven major league managers, but the quiet Carrigan remained his favorite skipper.

As the 1917 season opened, America declared war on Germany. Ruth registered for the military draft, but single men were called up first. The Babe did not expect to have to serve his country and he focused his energies on baseball. Off the field, Ruth's tremendous appetite continued to amaze everyone who watched him inhale a meal.

Tales of his feats at the table became as legendary as his achievements on the diamond. Breakfast might consist of 18 eggs with steaks and chops.

While some enjoyed an ice cream cone, Babe consumed a gallon at one sitting. One of his favorite snacks was several pounds of raw hamburger.

Since leaving St. Mary's, his weight had climbed to 194 pounds. The Babe's meteoric rise as a successful pitcher with power at the plate had escaped no one's attention, including his own.

Ruth recognized his status as a star and the usually good natured Babe became more aggressive. His temper sprouted a hair trigger. If an umpire made a call he disagreed with, the Babe often exploded.

On June 23, he took the mound in Boston to face Washington's first batter, Ray Morgan. When plate umpire

The tough kid from Baltimore began to dress well once he got to the big leagues.

Brick Owens called Babe's first pitch a ball, Ruth objected. Owens called the second pitch a ball. The Babe yelled and the ump cautioned him. When his third pitch was ball three, Ruth jawed, "Open your eyes."

"It's too early for you to kick," shouted Owens. "Get in there and pitch!"

Ruth responded by spiking the mound, making swiss cheese out of the hill. Seething, he delivered his fourth pitch.

"Ball four," barked Owens.

Stalking toward the plate, Babe challenged the umpire. "Why don't you open your . . . eyes?"

Accustomed to loud-mouth pitchers, Owens yelled back, "Get back out there and pitch or I'll run you out of the game."

"You run me out of the game," threatened Ruth, "and I'll bust you in the nose."

That was the Babe's ticket to an early shower. "Get the . . . out of here!" screamed Owens. "You're through!"

Ruth charged the plate like a bull. The catcher, Chester Thomas, attempted to shield the umpire, but Ruth's left fist landed on the back of Owens's neck. It took two players and a policeman to pull Ruth off the ump.

Ernie Shore took the mound, replacing Ruth with Morgan on first. Morgan was thrown out trying to steal second. Shore retired the next 26 batters in order and was credited with pitching a perfect game.

Ruth was suspended for 10 days and fined $100 by American League president Ban Johnson.

The Red Sox failed to win the pennant, but Ruth ended the season with a 24-13 record and a .325 batting average, fourth highest in the American League behind Ty Cobb, George Sisler, and Tris Speaker. After just three years, the 22-year-old pitcher and hitter had established himself as a star. In every way, Babe was big league.

INNING SIX

King of the Red Sox

1918-1919

"They ask me what it was I hit and I tell them I don't know except it looked good."

arly in the 1918 season, Red Sox captain Harry Hooper sat in the dugout at Fenway Park with manager Ed Barrow. [Many teams designated a player to be the team's leader, giving him the title of captain.] Barrow, who managed while dressed in a suit and tie, looked out at the field from beneath the brim of his straw hat. The Red Sox had lost some players to injuries and reshuffling was needed. When Hooper suggested that Babe become an outfielder, Barrow shot back, "I'd be the laughingstock of baseball if I changed the best left-hander in the game into an outfielder."

Barrow's reaction was understandable, but Hooper argued his case. "We need outfielders, not pitchers. We think the fans come out to see Ruth hit, so why not put him in the outfield every day?"

Hooper's words rang true. When Ruth pitched, attendance soared like the Babe's home runs. Spectators were willing to lay down their hard-earned money to watch Babe at the plate. Before the advent of television, baseball revenues were entirely dependent upon gate receipts, and attracting crowds was the name of the game. Hooper knew that Barrow had invested his own money in the Red Sox. The captain wisely pointed out that when attendance was up, so were the team's profits. Suddenly, he had Barrow's attention.

Baseball has always been a business. Ruth drew crowds wherever Boston played. Although Barrow hated to lose a solid starting pitcher, increasing ticket sales was more important. Thus, on May 6, 1918, Ruth started his first game as a fielder. Barrow started Babe at first base, then moved him to the outfield several days later. Ruth told a reporter, "Gee, it's lonesome in the outfield. It's hard to keep awake with nothing to do."

On his first appearance in left field, Babe went hitless, ending a 10-game hitting streak. A writer observed, "He didn't hit a thing, not even an umpire." But Babe's slump was brief and his bat soon ignited once more.

It was obvious to Barrow that he had a warhorse in Ruth. The Babe was young and strong. The manager, who believed his only job was to win, played Babe daily, and still put him on the mound when he needed a pitcher. Pitchers were expected to work nine full innings during Ruth's era. It was a matter of honor to "go the distance," and a hurler was disgraced if he could not complete nine innings. There were no set-up men, middle relievers or closers.

Babe soon grew tired. In addition to pitching entire games or playing the outfield daily, other factors contributed to his fatigue. Players wore flannel uniforms that absorbed their perspiration. At the end of a game, a sweat-soaked uniform could weigh 18 pounds. After pitching a complete game, Ruth felt like it weighed a ton. He complained to Barrow that he was being overworked, but the hard-nosed manager showed no pity.

The Red Sox skipper knew all about Babe's taste for the night life and believed that Ruth simply needed more rest. "Of course, you're tired," snapped Barrow. "That's because you're running around all the time. If you stopped your carousing at night and took better care of yourself, you could play every day and not feel it."

Late in the season, tragedy struck Ruth. Although Babe had traveled far from his home in Baltimore, he remained fond of his father. At the end of every season, he and Helen visited Mr. Ruth and helped out in the saloon. In late August, a customer and Babe's father got into a fight outside the bar. Mr. Ruth hit his head on the pavement and was killed. At 23, Babe had lost both his parents. Mamie, now married, was his only remaining family.

Babe ended the year hitting .300, playing first base in 13 games and in the outfield for 59 games. He pitched 20 games, and was 13-7. At the end of the war-shortened season, Boston captured the pennant, going on to take the World Series, 4 games to 2, from the Cubs. It was the Red Sox third World Championship in four years.

Two years earlier Ruth had held the Dodgers scoreless for the last 13 innings he faced them. When he shut out the Cubs 1-0 in Game 1 of the 1918 Series, his scoreless streak reached 22 innings. In Game 4 he shut them out for seven innings before giving up two runs in the eighth of a 3-2 win. It was his third consecutive World Series victory. He had shut out National League teams for 29-2/3 straight innings, topping Hall of Famer Christy Mathewson's record of 28. Babe's record would stand for 43 years, and although the world remembers him as the game's greatest slugger, Babe remained a pitcher at heart. He was prouder of his pitching record than any other.

The Red Sox had a good thing in Babe. Consequently, his salary had improved dramatically over the past several seasons, fattened by World Series bonuses. As his wealth increased, Ruth discovered the race track and also took up hunting. He and Helen traveled in the off-season.

The Babe with his first wife, Helen, and their adopted daughter, Dorothy.
They lived on a farm in Sudbury, Massachusetts.

They bought a farm near Boston where Babe enjoyed the outdoors, chopping wood to strengthen his pitching arm. But his new fame and wealth did not cause Babe to forget the people who had helped him along the way. He bought Brother Mathias a new Cadillac every year and he returned to St. Mary's as often as possible, always taking time to play ball with the boys.

When the war ended in November 1918, the country looked to the future with renewed optimism. Babe shared the nation's bright outlook. He realized the important role he played for the Red Sox. In turn, he expected to be paid for his star status.

No one doubted that the Babe was the king of the Bosox. The fans had come to adore him, cheering wildly whenever he stepped up to the plate. He thrilled them by the sight, sound, and sting of his bat on the leather.

It was worth the price of admission to see him strike out. When he missed, he cut an audible swath through the summer air. A newspaper writer said, "When Ruth misses a swipe at the ball, the stands quiver." His teammates and opponents alike were in awe of his power.

The Red Sox loved Babe's warm, friendly personality. Just a few years earlier, the veterans had sawed off the brash young rookie's bats, but that was in the past. Now, his teammates showed the Babe their affection, ribbing him with good-natured teasing.

While Babe clowned and joked a lot, he was no fool. "A

The Boston Red Sox were the best team in baseball during the Babe's time with them, and he was perhaps the best lefthanded pitcher in the game.

man ought to get all he can earn," Ruth said. "A man knows he's making money for other people and ought to get some of the profit he brings in. Don't make any difference if it's baseball or a bank or a vaudeville show. It's business."

In those days, baseball players did not have agents. Instead, they negotiated their own salaries with the owners. Contracts were usually for one year and were based on a player's performance during the past season. If an owner and player could not reach an agreement, the only bargaining tool a player possessed was to "hold out," not reporting to spring training until the requested salary had been met. Eventually, the player had to accept what the owner offered or get out of baseball. Players were bound to one team and were prohibited from playing for another club unless traded.

When salary negotiations began for the 1919 season, Ruth demanded a three-year contract at $10,000 a year, one of the top salaries in the game. Boston's owner, Harry Frazee, agreed.

Manager Barrow did not know how to handle the Babe as smoothly as Brother Mathias and Bill Carrigan had done. To Ruth, the crusty manager was a constant thorn in his side. Babe still bristled at rules. Barrow often sat in the hotel lobby, waiting for players to come in and fining them for breaking curfews. In Washington, the manager waited up for Ruth one night until he was exhausted. Finally Barrow went to bed, asking a hotel employee to let him know when Ruth came in.

At 6:00 A.M., someone knocked on Barrow's door. The Babe had just returned. Furious, the manager stomped down the hall in his robe and slippers. Ruth's door was unlocked. Barrow charged in to discover Babe lying in bed. The covers were pulled up to his chin and a pipe protruded from his mouth.

"Do you always smoke a pipe at this hour of the morning?" barked Barrow.

"Oh sure," responded Babe. "It's very relaxing."

Barrow was not amused. He yanked the covers off, revealing a fully-clothed Ruth, shoes and all.

Before that day's game, Barrow held a meeting. He lectured the men on team rules, focusing much of his talk on Ruth's bad habits. The Babe listened for a while, until he had heard enough. Humiliated and angry, he jumped up, threatening to punch the manager in the nose. Barrow suggested they close the clubhouse and have it out, man to man. The players were stunned. It seemed that time stopped as they waited to see how Ruth would respond.

It was never the Babe's style to back down. But Barrow was over 50 and Ruth may have thought of his own father's recent death caused by fighting. Whatever the reason, Babe slowly put on his uniform, taking the field for batting practice. But Babe never played that day. Barrow suspended him.

As the Red Sox train headed home through the night, a humbled Babe made his way to Barrow's room and asked to see him. "I'm awfully sorry about what happened today," said Ruth.

"You ought to be," responded the manager.

Perhaps Babe feared his father's fate would be his own. "Ed, some day somebody is going to kill me," he confessed.

Barrow was no soft touch, but he smiled. "Nobody's going to kill you, Babe. But don't you think it's time you straightened out and started leading a decent life now? You can't go on the way you've been going."

The two men compromised. Ruth suggested that he would leave a note in the manager's hotel mailbox, telling his skipper what time he got in. In return, he asked that Barrow stop leaning on him and lift the suspension. The system worked. When asked about it later, Barrow admitted, "I never checked up on him again. I took his word."

For the remainder of his career, Babe was famous for his night-time activities. He continued to ignore rules and managers. But there was one difference between Ruth and most mortals. He could stay out all night and play better than anyone had ever played the game the following day. No one could argue that.

Babe continued to play the outfield in 1919. And when the Red Sox got in a pitching jam, he came to the rescue, taking the mound 13 times. He hit .322 with 29 home runs, more than anyone had ever hit, launching homers in every city where the Red Sox played, another first. The rest of the team hit a total of four homers.

Before World War I, the home run was not an important part of baseball. Home runs were viewed as a cheap way of winning. Baseball strategists like Giants manager John McGraw emphasized walks, base-stealing, bunting, and manufacturing runs with sacrifices and plays like the hit and run. His New York team had stolen a record 347 bases in 1911. Players choked up on the bat, slapped or pushed or bunted the ball to get on base, moved along and scored on a hit-and-run or stolen base or ground ball. They seldom struck out. Taking a called third strike could yield a heavy fine from the manager. They tried to outwit their opponent, not outslug him. In fact, a batter who swung for the fences was considered selfish and not smart enough to play the game the way it was supposed to be played.

Baseball was an aggressive sport not meant for the faint-hearted. Although base running was an important part of the game, batting and running gloves did not exist. Players grasped fists full of dirt to prevent their hands from being scraped as they slid into base. Babe Ruth hit every home run in his career by clasping the bat with his bare hands.

Before Ruth's bat changed the game with the long ball, Frank "Home Run" Baker of the Athletics had led the league in homers for four years, never hitting more than 12. No one had ever hit like Babe. When players, managers, and fans saw him drive in so many runs with the round trippers, the home run took on a new meaning. The sight of Ruthian homers arcing and soaring against the summer sky thrilled

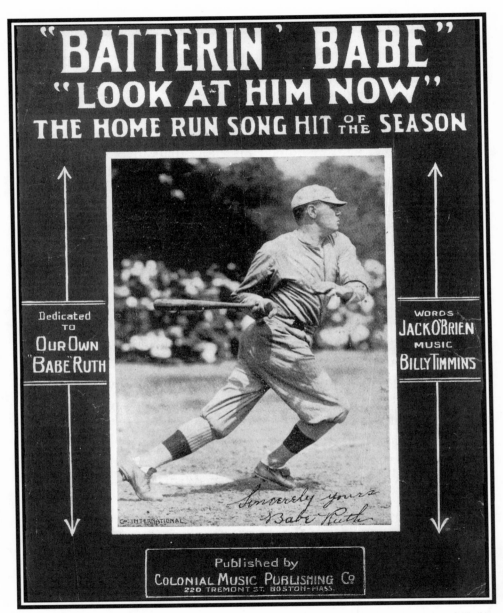

The Babe's reputation as a hitter began while he was with Boston. This is the first commercial notice of Babe the slugger.

players and fans alike. Suddenly, everyone was asking Babe how he did it. "All I can tell them is pick a good one and sock it," Ruth said. "I get back to the dugout and they ask me what it was I hit and I tell them I don't know except it looked good."

Despite Babe's popularity and his slugging, Boston finished a dismal sixth in 1919. Owner Harry Frazee, who also produced Broadway shows, was in financial trouble. He needed cash to launch a new show. Frazee decided to sell the player who would bring the highest price: the Babe.

The Yankees were shopping for talent that winter. The ball club had never fielded a winning team; compared to the New York Giants, the Yankees were a sorry excuse for a team, but they hoped to remedy that situation by investing in a slugger.

Since the team began in 1903, the Yankees had been owned by a pair of local politicians with little money to spend. In 1915, they sold the team for $460,000 to a pair of millionaires, Col. Jacob Ruppert, who owned a brewery, and Capt. Tillinghast L'Hommedieu Huston, a soldier-engineer.

Ruppert, who eventually bought out his partner, was a member of New York society, owned race horses, showed St. Bernards, attended the opera and served four terms in Congress. He and Huston liked to win and had the money to back up their desire.

Frazee had Ruth and wanted cash. Ruppert and Huston had the cash and wanted Ruth. They got him on December 26, 1919, for $100,000. Ruppert also made a personal loan of $350,000 to Frazee, taking a mortgage on Fenway Park. To this day, New York fans are still thanking Frazee. And to this day, Boston fans still dispise him.

Many Bostonians claim that Ruth's sale to the Yankees put a hex on the Red Sox. They have never won a World Series since 1918, when Babe pitched them to the championship. Three generations of Red Sox fans have suffered under "the curse of the Bambino."

Babe hit 54 home runs during his first season with the Yankees in 1923.

INNING SEVEN

The Bambino

1920-1923

"I try to make mush of the handle. The harder
you grip the bat, the faster the ball will travel."

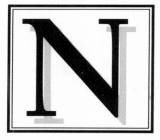

ew York City boasted three baseball teams in 1920: the American League Yankees and the National League Giants and Brooklyn Dodgers. It seemed that every New Yorker was a baseball fan devoutly loyal to one of the three teams. Men, women, and children filled the city's ballparks to root for their favorite clubs. Fans attended games dressed in their finest clothes, putting their best foot forward for the home team.

The Brooklyn Dodgers played at Ebbets Field. The Yankees shared the Giants' ball park, the horseshoe-shaped Polo Grounds; as one club traveled, the other team hosted home games. The Polo Grounds, located in a thin upper neck of Manhattan, was surrounded by tall apartment buildings.

Loyal fans of both teams came by subway, on the elevated train, or by foot. It was New York's glorious age of baseball. For eight of the next nine years, at least one New York team would play in the World Series.

The Dodgers had won a pennant in 1916, but John McGraw's Giants dominated the scene. McGraw, an international celebrity, was the most famous manager in baseball. He had built the Giants into America's richest and most famous sports team, mirroring his own dynamic personality. From 1903 to 1919, the Giants won six National League pennants and finished lower than second only four times. During the same period, the woeful Yankees never won a pennant. Ruppert was determined to change all that.

Like peanuts and Crackerjacks, many things about baseball are timeless, but the game was very different in that era. For instance, all major league baseball games were played during the day. In New York, games began at 3:00 P.M. or later to accommodate the work schedules of such diverse groups as Wall Street businessmen and Broadway theater workers. Games lasted about two hours, not three hours plus as they do today. Baseball was much more fast-paced with few pitching changes and little time-wasting at the plate. Batters just stepped up and swung, taking few time outs and staying in the box.

Ruth spent the winter of 1920 in California playing exhibition games and golfing. St. Mary's Industrial School had recently suffered a fire and the school was raising funds to rebuild. Babe arranged for the St. Mary's band to accompany the team on the tour to raise money for the school's new construction. He reported to the Yankees spring training camp at Jacksonville, Florida in February tan, fit, and lean, weighing 200 pounds. His New York teammates, glad Ruth was sporting pinstripes, immediately liked the jovial, fun-loving Babe.

Ping Bodie, Babe's roommate, was as good-natured as Ruth, and the amicable pair shared a love for food. Before Ruth's arrival, Bodie had held the distinction of having the heftiest appetite of any Yankee. But once Babe came on board, Bodie conceded his title to the ravenous

Ruth. "Anybody who eats three pounds of steak and a bottle of chili sauce for a starter has got me," admitted Bodie. The two men also clowned and joked like kids at summer camp. One day, the stocky, 5 foot 8 Bodie cut in front of Babe to field a grounder. Pretending to be angry, Ruth easily picked up his 195-pound roommate, turned him upside down, and dumped him on the grass like a sack of potatoes.

Three Yankee sluggers in 1921, from left to right, Ruth, Frank "Home Run" Baker, and Bob Meusel. A decade before, Baker had won homer titles with totals of 9, 10, 11 and 12.

Ruth was such an athletic phenomenon that scientists hooked him up to study his reflexes.

But no one cared if Babe clowned around because when he stepped up to the plate, Ruth was all business. The Yankees' lineup was already full of heavy hitters and had been dubbed Murderer's Row when they hit 45 home runs as a team in 1919. Adding Ruth, who had hit 29 himself, gave them a powerful punch. It remained to be seen if Babe could repeat that feat; some experts seriously doubted his ability to top his own record.

Babe started the season in a miserable hitting slump punctuated by numerous strikeouts. To worsen matters, the Red Sox humiliated the Yankees at Fenway during their first series of the year, sweeping them in a three-game stand. The Red Sox were hot, leading the league with a 10-2 record, and the Boston sportswriters felt smug. After all, they had predicted that the Bosox would be better off without the demanding, party-boy Babe. Ruth's cool bat only supported their recorded pearls of wisdom.

New York hoped to roust the Red Sox when Boston visited the Polo Grounds for the first time that season on Friday, April 30 for a five-game series. But Boston rubbed salt in the Yankees' open wound by defeating them once again in the first game.

Fans packed the Polo Grounds the following day. From every neighborhood in New York's sprawling metropolis, they made the pilgrimage to their cathedral of baseball to worship in the fresh air and sunshine for a few hours. Just a month earlier, new hope lived in the heart of every Yankee fan. Much of that hope centered on the Babe. Although it was still early in the season, the fans were growing increasingly skeptical about Ruth's potential.

It was Saturday May 1, 1920, May Day. The ancient Romans celebrated the day as heralding the official arrival of spring. Suddenly, it seemed that the ancient gods smiled down on Ruth. Babe stepped up to the plate. The stands and the diamond were alive with chatter as fans and players supported their teams with a constant stream of lively words. Unlike today, most managers did not sit in the dugout while their team batted. Instead, they occupied the coach's box at third base where, like generals, they commanded their troops, giving signals and offering encouragement to the batters and base runners. Manager Miller Huggins called to Babe from his post at third, "Come on, big boy!"

With a loud crack that pierced the spring air, Ruth responded by hitting his first home run of the year, a majestic drive soaring over the Polo Grounds roof. The fans were wild with excitement. Just as he had thrilled the crowd, the Babe's bat also ignited his team; before the Red

Sox train left New York, the Yankees had taken three of the five games.

The Red Sox never recovered, finishing the season in fifth place. But the Yankees were on their way, hitched to Ruth's rising star. The crack of Babe's bat had signaled the beginning of the Yankee dynasty and a new age for baseball.

Before May ended, Babe had slammed 12 home runs, more than any player had ever hit in one month. Yankee fans celebrated with a joyous frenzy of excitement. On May 16, a record crowd of 38,600 jammed the Polo Grounds and 15,000 were turned away at the gate. Police patrolled the seemingly endless line of fans hoping to buy a treasured ticket to catch a golden glimpse of Ruth at the plate and take a piece of Babe's magic back to their ordinary lives.

The Yankees stayed in a hot three-way pennant race with Chicago and Cleveland that was marred by one tragic incident. On August 16, Ruth was in the outfield at Cleveland when the Indians shortstop, Ray Chapman, was struck below the left ear by a pitch thrown by Yankee hurler Carl Mays. "The blow cracked poor Ray's skull," remembered Babe, "and he died the next day."

Chapman is the only player ever killed in a major league game. (Batting helmets were not introduced until the early 1950s.)

Later that month, when the team returned to New York, Babe began filming a movie, "The Babe Comes Home." He was the toast of the town. Songs were written about him and, whenever baseball was mentioned, so was the Babe.

By October, Ruth had hit an astounding 54 home runs, more than any other *team* in the league, while batting .376. He packed ballparks throughout the country; the Yankees, who finished third, outdrew the Giants at the Polo Grounds by more than 350,000 fans. Fans who had once ignored the presence of the Yankees now flocked to see the Babe. For the first time his home runs captured the biggest headlines. John McGraw's Giants became the "other" team in town. In 1919, the

Yankees attendance had been 619,164. With Ruth in 1920, it doubled to 1,289,422. Ironically, it was McGraw who had suggested Ruppert buy the once floundering Yankees. Now they had become the Giants' turnstile rival.

New York was America's largest and most glamorous city. A vast, simmering meltingpot of cultural and ethnic groups, everything in the city was big time: newspapers, fancy restaurants, theaters, and endless trendy nightlife. New Yorkers were also known for their unique charac-

Babe Ruth always seemed ready for any sort of fun—especially with kids. Here he wears a cap and plays a horn from the St. Mary's band before a game in Philadelphia.

ter, a combination of style tinged with toughness. Larger than life and a bit rough around the edges, Ruth fit perfectly in the New York scene. He had found his home. To signal their affection for Babe, the city's large Italian population called him "Bambino" (Italian for baby).

Ruth's teammates loved him, too. As the club traveled around the league by train, Babe and his fellow Yankees enjoyed endless hours of card-playing and storytelling. With his everpresent cigar in hand, Ruth laughed and joked with everyone. To supplement the dining car's fare, he provided mounds of his favorite foods for the team—large platters of ribs and gallons of ice cream. Babe gladly shared his gifts just as he had done as a kid at St. Mary's.

The Babe with his manager, Miller Huggins. He tormented the little skipper until Huggins fined him $5,000.

Not only did his teammates and New Yorkers love the Babe, the entire country had found a hero. Not since President Teddy Roosevelt had such a figure emerged to inspire the nation, capturing the country's imagination and heart. Americans were fascinated by Babe's achievements in baseball and the joy he brought to the game, but they also respected the slugger for his dedication to children. Ruth always made time for kids, signing autographs, posing for pictures, or visiting orphanages and hospitals. With the Babe, there was never a sense that his appearances were public relations ploys. Instead, he conveyed a warmth and sincerity that endeared him to the nation.

The admiration that fans felt for Ruth helped to save the game from a tragic event that threatened to erode baseball's integrity in 1920. Following the 1919 World Series between Cincinnati and Chicago, it was alleged that eight of the White Sox players had accepted bribes to lose the contest to the Reds. The incident quickly became known as the "Black Sox" scandal. Although the courts never convicted any of the eight players, Baseball Commissioner Kenesaw Mountain Landis banned the players for life. Babe's feats that season helped the nation to focus on the positive aspects of baseball, turning their attention away from the potentially ruinous scandal that rocked the sport.

Babe was now a New Yorker. He and Helen lived in an apartment in the city's posh Astoria Hotel, but they kept their Sudbury farm near Boston and spent much time there in the off-season. In February 1921, the couple adopted an infant daughter, Dorothy.

Propelled by Babe's bat, the Yankees skyrocketed that season. Babe drew 144 walks, scored 177 runs and drove in 170. He proved that his power at the plate was no fluke, topping his own home run record with 59. When he'd hit 29 home runs in 1919, it was considered by many experts to be a freak occurrence, unlikely to be matched. But when he hit 54, then 59, he changed forever the style of batting and the attitude of the players, who equated his popularity and high salary with his home runs, and tried to emulate him.

Baseball had suddenly changed. John McGraw recognized the new era and gradually adapted to it. But Ty Cobb, the greatest of the scientific ballplayers, whose supremacy in the game was now challenged by Ruth, disliked the slugger and the slugging game intensely. For 15 years Cobb had been baseball's biggest star. No more.

One day Cobb told two sportswriters that he could hit home runs too, if he really tried. That day he hit three, plus a double and two singles. The next day he hit two more out of the park. Then, having proven his point, he went back to hitting singles and doubles and stealing his way around the basepaths. Cobb was not about to become a part of the home run fad.

Pioneer sportswriter Henry Chadwick, often called the "father of baseball" because he created the modern box score and scoring methods, had decried the home run decades earlier:

"…what attractive feature does it add to the game compared with the chances for fielding skill which it deprives the fielder of?…Just think of the monotony of a game marked by a series of home runs in each inning."

But the fans did not agree with Cobb or Chadwick. They loved the long ball and the man who changed the sport, George Herman Ruth. No one has ever come close to Babe's slugging averages of .847 and .846 for the 1920 and '21 seasons. (A batting average is calculated by hits divided by times at bat; a slugging average is determined by total bases divided by times at bat. It is a measure of a hitter's power.)

In 1920 the slugging game exemplified by Ruth had been aided by changes in the pitching rules. Before this time, pitchers used the same ball for most of a game. During a 1916 game between the Cubs and the Reds one ball was used for the entire game. As the innings progressed, it became dirty and lopsided. The hitters had difficulty seeing the dark, soft lump. It had been a common practice for some pitchers to doctor the ball, spraying it with tobacco juice, scraping it with emery, nicking or cutting it, and stuffing mud into the seams. A drop of sweat or spit on the ball could make it dart and weave and drop unpredictably. The spitball was now outlawed, along with any acts that defaced the ball. More new, white, shiny balls were used in each game. Hitters could simply see the ball better and blasted it farther and more frequently.

In 1921, New York captured its first American League pennant, and the Yankees faced their Polo Grounds landlords, the Giants, in the World Series. It was the first Series to be played entirely in one ball-park.

"That first flag was like the first of 15 children," Babe reflected. "It was wonderful! New York had been waiting 18 years for its first American League pennant and the town went wild, especially as the Giants had won that season in the National League."

Check the size of the Babe's glove. "Two hands" wasn't just for beginners in those days!

The Yankees fought valiantly during the eight-game Series, but the Giants defeated their hometown rivals, 5-3. [In the first World Series in 1903, it took 5 victories to win the championship. Then the format was changed to 4 out of 7, and remained that way until 1919, when it was changed back to 5 wins. This remained in effect for three years; since 1922 the present 4 out of 7 format has been used.]

Babe batted .313 with one homer and four RBI. Despite losing the Series, everyone sensed that the tide had turned for the Yankees.

"Up until the time I came to New York it was pretty much of a National League town," Ruth wrote in his autobiography. But now Babe was on the scene and there was always next season.

Although players earned good salaries compared to other professions, their incomes were modest when measured against today's standards. Ballplayers worked a second job in the off-season to earn an adequate income. Some players supplemented their salaries by barnstorming, touring the country with a team of big leaguers playing exhibition games in cities and towns. But there was one hitch. Players who had been in the World Series were prohibited from barnstorming.

True to his nature, Ruth ignored the rule following the 1921 Series. However, Judge Landis, the Commissioner of Baseball, did not ignore the infraction. He slapped Ruth and his teammate, Bob Meusel, with a 30-day suspension. The two Yankees didn't start the 1922 season until May 20. But when Babe began playing, the club honored him by making him the team captain.

Following the suspension, Ruth played poorly. After five days, his average stood at .093 and the fans loudly booed him. The Bambino had fallen from grace. On May 25 at the Polo Grounds, he tried to stretch a single into a double and was thrown out at second. Frustrated by the call, he threw a handful of dirt into the umpire's

Baseball Commissioner Kenesaw Mountain Landis suspended Ruth and Bob Meusel when they barnstormed against his orders.

face. His gesture earned him a trip to the showers, his first ejection as a Yankee.

Babe walked toward the dugout accompanied by loud jeers from the fans. Nearing the bench, he stopped, removed his cap, and sarcastically bowed to the booing throng. A man behind the dugout called out, "You . . . big bum, why don't you play ball?"

Ruth plunged into the stands after the man, but other fans restrained him. Another fan yelled, "Hit the big stiff!"

Suddenly, Babe's rough street-kid roots emerged. He shook his fist at the crowd. "Come on down and fight!" he yelled. "Anyone who wants to fight come down on the field! Aw, you're all alike, you're all yellow."

Following the game, Ruth told a reporter, "I didn't mean to hit the umpire with the dirt, but I did mean to hit that [bum] in the stands. If I make a home run every time I bat, they'd think I'm all right. If I don't, they think they can call me anything they like . . . I'll go into the stands again if I have to."

League president Ban Johnson suspended Ruth for one game and fined him $200 following the incident. "Dust on umpires happens in the heat of the moment," Johnson said, "but we cannot condone anyone going into the stands." The Yankees also stripped Ruth of his coveted role as the team's captain, a position he had held for just five days. It was a bitter blow to the Babe.

The Yankees played 154 games that year, but Ruth appeared in only 110. He was suspended for fighting again and he was sidelined with the flu. However, the Yankees still won the pennant and faced the Giants once again in the World Series. But the dark cloud continued to hover over Babe during the Series when he batted a dismal .118. The Giants took the crown in a four-game sweep.

Although Babe's stats for 1922 remained impressive (he batted .315 and hit 35 homers), his numbers had plummeted from the prior sea-

Especially in his younger days, Babe was a good fielder, with a strong, accurate arm from the outfield.

son. In the span of one brief year, Ruth had fallen from golden boy to whipping boy. Fans had accepted Ruth's reputation as a party-boy when he was hitting, but they resented his partying if he could not deliver at the plate.

Stories of Babe's off-the-field antics were widespread. Over the years, he had wrecked cars and wound up in countless scrapes, but he had usually escaped both trouble and harm. Now Babe was being held accountable for his performance. Fans and management cited his poor physical condition and blamed him for not respecting himself and his team.

At a dinner that winter in New York, the city's future mayor, James J. Walker, delivered a speech confronting Babe about his lack of responsibility. Walker talked about the "dirty-faced kids" who looked up to Ruth. Looking at Babe, he asked, "Are you going to keep on letting those little kids down?"

The Babe was visibly moved. Until that moment, no one had been able to reason with him, but Walker's words touched Ruth's soul. Memories of his own childhood welled inside his rough exterior. He knew the role that St. Mary's, Brother Mathias, and baseball had played in his life. Babe had made mistakes and he knew it, but now he had an opportunity to show everyone what he was really made of.

That night, Babe publicly vowed to change his ways. "I know as well as anybody else just what mistakes I made last season," he confessed. "There's no use in me trying to get away from them. But let me tell you something. I want the New York sportswriters and fans to know that I've had my last drink until next October. I mean it. Tomorrow I'm going off to my farm. I'm going to work my head off—and maybe part of my stomach."

The audience laughed. "I'm serious about this," countered Babe. "I'm going to work hard. And then you just watch me break that home run record next year."

INNING EIGHT

The House that Ruth Built

1923-1928

"Kids will be hitting them there when I'm gone, I'm kind of glad I hit the first one."

arly in the 1922 season, the Giants had served the Yankees with an eviction notice. Resenting the Yankees' superior attendance, the Giants recommended the Yanks build their own park. The Yankees gladly obliged, erecting a magnificent new stadium across the Harlem River in the Bronx just a half-mile from the Polo Grounds. Construction began in 1922 and the new facility was ready for the 1923 season. The 62,000-seat Yankee Stadium was the largest existing baseball park and it was a stunning structure. Much to the chagrin of the Giants, the Yankees now had Babe Ruth and a huge new stadium packed with fans who soon pegged their club the Bronx Bombers.

Ruth honored his pledge to mend his ways in 1923. He reported to spring training in good shape, weighing in at 215 pounds. When Yankee Stadium opened on April 18, 1923, Ruth hit a 3-run homer to defeat the Red Sox, 4 to 1. The Yankees took the 1923 pennant, boosted by Babe's .393 batting average and 41 home runs. An excellent baserunner, he also stole 17 bases. Wary pitchers, afraid of his bat, walked him a record 170 times. They would prefer to see him on first base rather than blasting another one over the fence.

For the third consecutive year, the Yankees faced the Giants in the World Series, but this time the contest was staged in two different stadiums. Because fans traveled by subway to both ballparks, the contest became known as the first "Subway Series." The Yankees finally took the crown with the help of Babe, who walloped three homers. Back on top again, Ruth was a unanimous choice for Most Valuable Player in the American League. Babe and the country had learned a lasting les-

The Babe didn't always poke one out and jog around the bases. Here he slides across the plate at Yankee Stadium.

son: even heroes make mistakes, but the true measure of a man is what is in his heart. Babe had kept his promise to the "dirty-faced kids," to the Yankees, and most important, to himself.

Ruth's popularity and fame made him a natural for endorsing commercial products. There was the Babe Ruth Cigar, and his picture appeared on cereal boxes. When Babe Ruth's Home Run Candy appeared, the Curtiss Candy Corporation cried foul. They already produced a candy bar called Baby Ruth, named for President Grover Cleveland's daughter, Ruth. Curtiss appealed to the Patent Office and Babe was forced to pull his product.

The following season, Babe led the league with a .378 average and 46 home runs. But despite his heroic efforts, the Washington Senators took the 1924 pennant.

In 1925, when the 30-year-old Babe reported for spring training, he weighed 250 pounds. Even worse, he was ill, still suffering from the effects of a serious case of flu. As the team headed north, Babe collapsed in the train station at Asheville, North Carolina.

The Yankees traveled on, but Babe remained in Asheville, where he rested. Arriving in New York, he fainted on the train and was rushed to St. Vincent's Hospital on April 9, where he underwent abdominal surgery. Rumors of his death circulated; later the illness was called "the bellyache heard round the world."

Ruth's critics claimed he was washed up, his career over. When he rejoined the club, he hit only .290 with 25 home runs. The Yankees plummeted to seventh place. To make matters worse, Babe resumed his nightlife during a road trip, ignoring Manager Miller Huggins's curfew. Huggins was thoroughly disgusted with Ruth's poor performance. In St. Louis, he hit Ruth with a $5,000 fine and suspended him, claiming that Ruth disobeyed orders both on and off the field. He told Babe to pack his bags and go back to New York.

Angry words flew between Huggins and Ruth. Babe reacted with his usual street-kid tact, threatening to slug Huggins. Six inches shorter, 100 pounds lighter, and 15 years older than Ruth, Huggins drove home his points by repeatedly jabbing his finger in Babe's ample chest. "If I were half your size, I'd have punched you," Huggins declared. "And I'll tell you something else, mister. Before you get back in uniform, you're going to apologize for what you've said, and apologize plenty."

Seething, Babe vowed to take his case to the Commissioner of Baseball. He complained to the press, claiming that Huggins was making him a scapegoat by blaming him for the team's weak showing. But the Yankees backed Huggins and Ruth later apologized to his manager in New York. "I'm hotheaded," he said lamely. Like a thoroughbred chomping at the bit, Babe longed to play, but Huggins wisely allowed Ruth to stew in his own juice. Finally, after nine days, Huggins put him back in the lineup. As if to celebrate, Babe hit his 300th career home run the next day.

As Ruth's fame and legend grew, so did the numbers of fans who flocked after him. In fact, Babe was like the "Pied Piper of Baseball."

Ruth's first game back after 1925's "bellyache heard 'round the world."

But he never tried to avoid the crowds. Instead, Babe loved children like no one else who ever played baseball. Perhaps it was because he remained a big kid himself.

One day Ruth and his family were driving home from Yankee Stadium following a long, sweltering doubleheader. They stopped at a red light and Babe saw a group of kids playing baseball. The kids also spotted Babe. Instantly, a hoard of children descended on the car. To their delight, Babe, who was wearing a white flannel suit and silk shirt, emerged from the vehicle. "Come on," begged the children. "Let's see you hit a few." For the next 30 minutes, as Ruth's family waited patiently in the car, Babe thrilled the kids by hitting easy flies they could shag, giving them a memory to last a lifetime.

Pitcher Waite Hoyt described how everyone, children and adults, adored the Babe. "I've seen what he did to people! I've seen them, fans driving miles in open wagons through the prairies of Oklahoma to see him in exhibition games as we headed north in the spring," wrote Hoyt.

"I've seen them: kids, men, women, worshippers all, hoping for a grunt of recognition when they said, 'H'ya Babe.' He never let them down; not once! He was the greatest crowd pleaser of them all. It wasn't so much that

Babe poses for photographers at his Sudbury farm.

*The Babe connects for one of his four home runs against the Cardinals in
the 1926 World Series. He hit three in one game.*

he hit home runs, it was how he hit them and the circumstances under
which he hit them."

Babe, the Yankees' prodigal son, reported to spring training in 1926
fit and lean. During the winter he had dieted and exercised, shedding
35 pounds. He had also spent the off-season apologizing once more.
"I'm going to make good all over again," he vowed. "I used to get sore
when people called me a sap and tried to steer me right . . .But all
those people were right. Now, though, I know that if I am to wind up
sitting pretty on the world, I've got to face the facts and admit that I
have been the sappiest of saps."

One of Ruth's 1926 World Series homers crashed through the window of an auto dealer across the street from the ballpark.

Many doubted the sincerity of Ruth's words, but when they saw him in such excellent condition, they admitted he again looked like the Bambino of old. By this time, no one underestimated Babe. However, the experts were skeptical about the 1926 Yankees, predicting they would finish fourth. Several young players reported to camp that spring, including two rookies, Tony Lazzeri and Mark Koenig, and a promising first base prospect named Lou Gehrig. Gehrig's parents were German, like Ruth's, and the two players struck up a friendship. Babe spent many hours at the Gehrigs' home, feasting on Mom Gehrig's excellent German cooking.

The Babe caught a ball dropped from an airplane in 1926.

Later that season, the Bronx Bombers silenced their critics by clinching the pennant. Babe ended the season with 47 homers and a .372 batting average, not too bad for a guy who was supposedly washed up.

During the season, Babe had befriended Johnny Sylvester, a bedridden 11-year-old boy who had been crippled by a bone disease. He asked both World Series teams to send

Johnny autographed baseballs, but Babe sent the boy something even more special. Babe wrote Johnny a note: "I'll hit a home run for you in Wednesday's game."

Babe did more than keep his promise. He hit not one, but three homers that day for Johnny. And although the Yankees bowed to the St. Louis Cardinals in a seven-game World Series battle, it did not matter to Johnny Sylvester. Two weeks after the Series, Babe again visited the boy.

Although Babe was enjoying a rejuvenated career, his marriage to Helen was over. She had spent most of their marriage alone at the couple's Sudbury farm. Babe had made no secret of his relationship with another woman, Claire Hodgson, an actress, but because he and Helen were Catholics, a divorce was out of the question. The couple merely separated and Dorothy, 5, remained with her mother.

For the first time in his career, Babe had a slugging competitor on his own bench in 1927. The young Lou Gehrig matched Ruth homer for homer from April to mid-August. In fact, Gehrig led Ruth, 38-35, on August 10. But then, Ruth astounded the nation. With the passing of each day, his home run pace quickened and he predicted he would break his own 1921 record of 59 round trippers. Many doubted it was possible.

But Babe was charging down the home stretch and, like a true champion, he could taste the sweetness of 60 homers. As Ruth hit each additional home run, collectors began to storm the field, hoping to swipe his bat. To frustrate them, Babe began to carry his bat as he jogged around the bases following each homer. Once a young boy ran on the field as Ruth rounded third. He grabbed Babe's bat and Ruth crossed home plate dragging the bat, the boy, and tons of excitement.

With only four games to go, he needed four home runs. He completed the feat in Ruthian style. Not only did Babe hit two grand slams, he belted his 60th home run on September 30, a day before the final game. After the game, his voice penetrated the clubhouse. "Sixty, count 'em, sixty! Let's see some other [sonofagun] match that!"

Any home run sailing beyond the fence is a sight to behold. No matter how old or how sophisticated a spectator becomes, the sight still causes one to return to childish wonder for an instant, suspending one's breath. Before the sight comes the sound: an unmistakable crack that sends adrenalin racing through the veins of the hitter, the players, and the fans.

Babe Ruth hit them like nobody else. The legend of a Ruthian homer lives today, not only because of their frequency, but because of the unique arc Babe's homers traced against the sky. If Ruth hit an inside pitch, the ball soared majestically, seeming to exit the park destined for orbit in some heavenly sphere. If Babe got a piece of something on the outside of the plate, the ball both curved and arced, cutting a blazing meteoric trail in America's memory. Today's homers average approximately 382 feet, but the "tale of the tape" is a relatively new phenomenon. No one thought to measure home runs in Babe's era.

One example of Ruth's mythical might was recorded in San Francisco. Babe had broken all his bats during a barnstorming tour. The heavy lumber Ruth swung was hard to come by; however, someone in San Francisco loaned him a 54-ounce bat. During a Saturday exhibition game at Seals Stadium, he sent a ball soaring out of the park. When it landed 150 feet beyond 14th Street, it just missed hitting a sign painter. It left a mark on the pavement and the painter marked the spot with a 12-inch by 12-inch square. On Sunday morning, the shot was measured using a chalk line to chart the course from home plate. One witness reported that the ball had traveled 714 feet.

Today, many baseball experts still claim that the 1927 Yankees were the best team to ever play the game. As a club, the Yankees batted .307, set a major league home run record, and won 110 games, dropping

Many baseball historians feel the 1927 Yankees were the greatest team in the sport's history. Babe stands fifth from left, top row.

The Babe watches number 60 headed for the seats, September 30, 1927.
The pitcher was Washington's Tom Zachary.

90

only 44. They won the pennant by 19 games. The club shared a special affection for one another. Babe's teammates fondly dubbed him "Jidge," an endearing form of George. Mom Gehrig even named her dog Jidge for her son's good friend.

One of the game's great one-two punches: Babe Ruth and Lou Gehrig. When the Yankees assigned numbers to their players, Ruth, who batted third, got number 3. Gehrig, who batted fourth, got number 4.

The Yankees traveled to Pittsburgh's Forbes Field to meet the Pirates in the World Series. Wilbert Robinson, manager of the Brooklyn Dodgers, sat in the stands, watching the Yankees take batting practice. Robinson had never seen such a display of pyrotechnics.

Predicting Pittsburgh's defeat, Robinson declared, "They're beaten already." Robinson proved to be a wise prophet. The Yankees made short work of Pittsburgh, sweeping them in four games.

Despite Babe's 60 home runs, he was not chosen the league's Most Valuable Player. Ruth had won the title in 1923 and a rule prohibited any player from winning the award twice.

In 1928, Connie Mack's Philadelphia A's challenged the mighty Bronx Bombers. Mack had assembled a formidable lineup, boasting the likes of Al Simmons, Mickey Cochrane, Jimmie Foxx, Lefty Grove, Ty Cobb and Tris Speaker. When the Yankees finally claimed the pennant, Philadelphia was still nipping at their heels, trailing by only 2 1/2 games. But the Yankees had an easier time in the Series, capturing the crown again in a four-game sweep of the Cardinals.

Babe and his teammates were walking in tall cotton. It was a magical time. Yankee fans hoped it would last forever.

Babe hit three homers in one game during the 1928 World Series—the second time he'd put on such a post-season show.

INNING NINE

The Final Innings

1929-1948
"I'm glad I can be here to thank everyone."

pril 17, 1929 was Opening Day for the Yankees. That morning, Babe and Claire Hodgson married. Helen Ruth, Babe's first wife, had died in a tragic fire in Boston earlier that year. Babe and his new bride were married at 6:00 A.M., hoping to avoid a large crowd at the wedding, but their plans didn't succeed. Thousands waited outside the church, including almost every photographer and writer in New York. As the couple emerged from the church, they were greeted by a shower of rice and rain. The newlyweds had planned to begin their marriage at the game at Yankee Stadium, but it was rained out and postponed until the next day. Babe and Claire had a ready-made family. She had a daughter from a previous marriage and Babe's daughter, Dorothy, also joined their household. The future looked bright.

During the 1929 season, the Yankees sported numbers on their uniforms for the first time, representing their spots in the lineup. Since

Babe batted third, he became number 3. (By 1937, every team had numbers on their uniforms.)

Another change occurred near the season's end. Manager Miller Huggins died suddenly and Babe was devastated. Although he and Huggins had not always seen eye-to-eye, Ruth loved and admired the crusty skipper. At 34, Babe hoped to be named manager, but the post was given to pitcher Bob Shawkey. When Shawkey was fired the following year, Babe again hoped to get the job. But Col. Ruppert knew

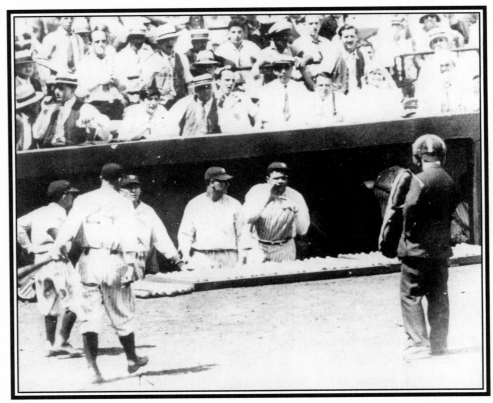

The Babe is infuriated after getting tossed out of a 1930 game for jawing at umpire Brick Owens.

too much about Babe's lack of discipline in his own affairs to believe he could manage effectively. The die was cast. The Yankees appointed Joe McCarthy, who had gained his experience managing the Chicago Cubs. Babe never liked McCarthy for one simple reason: the Yankees had made him the manager, not Ruth.

Babe was paying the price for the reputation he had earned as someone who ignored the rules. Realizing that his days were numbered as a player, he hoped to continue contributing to the game as a manager. But the Yankees did not share the Babe's vision. It was a hurt that would never heal.

From 1929 to 1931, the Philadelphia A's dominated the American League, aided by the bat of their great hitter, Jimmie Foxx. But Ruth kept right on slugging. On August 11, 1929, he hit his 500th home run and on August 21, 1931, he hit number 600.

In 1932, the Yankees mounted a comeback, outpacing the A's by 13 games for the pennant. Babe's weight had crept up over the years and his knees bothered him constantly, but he still managed to hit .341 with 41 home runs.

The Bronx Bombers faced the Cubs in the Series. Once again, the Yankees swept the Series in four games. But today the 1932 fall classic is best remembered for Ruth's controversial "Called Shot." It would be Babe's last World Series, but what a fitting exit for the Bambino.

America was in the throes of a devastating financial crisis called the Great Depression in the early 1930s. When the stock market crashed in 1929, the nation's economy collapsed, wiping out jobs and businesses. Hunger was a reality for millions. Once-proud workers suddenly roamed the street begging. Thousands waited in soup kitchen lines stretching across the crippled country.

Attendance at baseball games also nose-dived in some cities, almost destroying ball clubs. But because New York was such a vast metropolis, baseball fared better there than in most cities. Babe Ruth continued to pack Yankee Stadium. Indeed, over the years, Babe's presence paid for the cost of the stadium many times over. It was only fitting that the ball park became known as "The House that Ruth Built." The crowds he drew in every city helped to keep some American League teams in business.

Richards Vidmer, a New York sportswriter, described Babe's unequaled popularity: "If you weren't around in those times, I don't think you could appreciate what a figure the Babe was. He was bigger than the President. One time, coming north, we stopped at a little town in Illinois, a whistle stop. It was about ten o'clock at night and raining like hell. The train stopped for ten minutes to get water, or something. It couldn't have been a town of more than five thousand people, and by God, there were four thousand of them down there standing in the rain, just waiting to see the Babe."

On Long Island, a group of children stood at the edge of a golf course, watching Ruth play. Seeing the youngsters, he went over to shake their hands, accidentally stepping on one boy's toes. The other kids were eternally jealous because for the rest of his life that boy could say that the Babe had stepped on his foot.

In the midst of America's economic woes, Babe was earning an unprecedented salary of $80,000. During that same year, the next highest paid stars earned about $30,000, but the average salary among players was under $10,000. This was still twice as much as most working men earned. (United States senators were paid $10,000 a year.) When Vidmer wrote that Ruth was "bigger than the President," he was not joking. Babe's salary was $5,000 higher than President Herbert Hoover's. When a reporter pointed out this fact, Ruth did not apologize, "I know," he answered, "but I had a better year than Hoover."

Although most baseball players were not stars like the Babe, they all benefited from the raised salary levels. Players credited Ruth for improving their earnings and thanked him for it.

In a 1931 exhibition game in Chattanooga, Tennessee, Jackie Mitchell, a 17-year-old girl, used her sinker to strike out both Babe Ruth and Lou Gehrig. Chattanooga Lookouts owner Joe Engel is next to Ruth.

The first All-Star Game was played at Chicago's Comiskey Park in 1933. The brainchild of Chicago *Tribune* sports editor, Arch Ward, it was to be a one-time event held in connection with the 1933 Worlds Fair in Chicago. Profits from the first All-Star contest went toward the players' pension fund and a Chicago charity. The fans voted for the starting players. Connie Mack and the retired John McGraw were named the managers in recognition of their long careers as managers.

Comiskey Park was filled to capacity for the event on July 6. The architect who added the stadium's second deck had claimed, "No player will ever hit a ball out of this park." He had not seen the Babe. Ruth took a pitch over the roof that day, thrilling the Chicago crowd and spoiling the architect's ill-fated promise. The game was successful and was repeated for the next four years. But it did not become an official annual event until 1938.

During the final game of the 1933 season, Babe took the mound for the first time in three years. The 38-year-old southpaw shut Boston out for the first five innings. Although his arm stiffened, Babe went the dis-

In 1933, the first All-Star Game was held, and Babe hit the first home run. Even the White Sox batboy congratulated him.

tance, even hitting a home run to put the icing on the Yankees 6-5 win. An hour after the game had ended, fans still waited to cheer their hero. Ruth's smile revealed his delight, but he failed to acknowledge the fans' salute with the traditional tip of his cap. Babe could not even lift his sore left arm.

Despite the country's floundering economy, Ruth asked the Yankees for a pay hike in 1934. Amazingly, no one criticized Babe. Instead, the New York *Sun* defended the Bambino's contribution to America's spirit. Acknowledging

Gehrig and Ruth posing again.

that Ruth earned more than a state governor, a Supreme Court Judge, or college president, the paper declared that none of them "ever made 30,000 Americans spring up and make us forget yesterday and tomorrow for a moment, and you can name your price tag."

In 1934, Ruth's popularity was at its zenith. He had his own radio program and the "Babe Ruth Club" newspaper. That year, 50 boys who won a Babe Ruth essay contest enjoyed a trip to spring training camp, spending time with the Babe. He blasted his 700th home run at Detroit's Navin Field (now Tiger Stadium) on July 13. [It numbs the senses to realize that Ruth actually hit as many as 50 more homers that were canceled because of the rules of the time. The old rule stated that a ball was called foul if the umpires saw it hook into foul territory before it disappeared from view.]

But the aging veteran's body was protesting. Babe had injured his knees in 1919 and, after years of supporting his ballooning frame, they

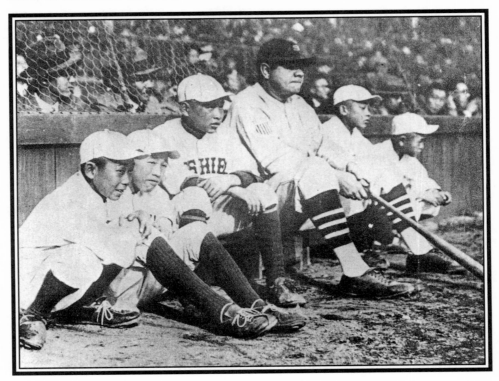

Babe poses with kids during 1934 tour of Japan.

stiffened and ached. As his age and weight gradually climbed, his stats slowly descended. That year he played in only 125 games, batting .288 and hitting just 22 round-trippers. Although Babe realized his career with the Yankees could not last forever, he was not yet ready to hang up the spikes. "Don't quit until every base is uphill," he had once said.

Babe and Claire joined a group of 14 players that Connie Mack assembled for an exhibition tour of Japan following the 1934 season. The 13 other players might as well have stayed at home. Ruth captured all the attention, as the Japanese trailed on his heels. After the trip, Babe and his wife went on to Paris. When the Ruths visited an

Contest winners got to visit the Yankees spring training camp in 1934 as guests of the Babe. Yankees owner Col. Jake Ruppert looks on.

American school there, Babe was shocked to learn that the children did not know how to play baseball. "Imagine an American kid not knowing how to swing a bat!" he declared.

When Ruth returned home, his thoughts turned to the upcoming season. Babe still longed to become a manager. At the end of the 1934 season, he had told a reporter that he would only return to the Yankees in a manager's role.

Ruth had backed the Yankees into a corner with his declaration. They had no management positions available. The club owner, Col. Jake Ruppert, was happy with his manager, Joe McCarthy, but he couldn't just dump the most popular man in the country. The National League Boston Braves bailed the Yankees out by offering Ruth a player-coach position, with an ambiguous promise of managing in the future. In February 1935 Ruppert handed Babe this notice that announced the end of his career with the club:

> Mr. George H. Ruth
> You are hereby notified as follows:
> 1. That you are unconditionally released.

The Braves were performing dismally and they hoped that Ruth's return to Boston would bolster their ailing attendance. Lured by the possibility of becoming a skipper, Ruth signed with the beleaguered Braves for the 1935 season.

In happier days, Ruth, with wife Claire, agrees to contract terms with Col. Ruppert.

With nicknames like "Sultan of Swat" and "King of Klout," the Babe sometimes dressed the part. Did any Royal Personage ever look better?

Babe still packed the parks, but his aching body made every play a painful ordeal. The bases were all uphill for Ruth, who was ready to quit. But Boston persuaded him to complete a farewell tour, visiting every city in the league. Each ballpark hosted a Babe Ruth Day and thousands turned out for a final glimpse of the Bambino.

In Pittsburgh, the Babe had his last big day with the bat. He thrilled the crowd with three home runs, driving in six runs. His last, number 714, was the first ever hit over the right field stands at Forbes Field. It was measured at 600 feet. A doubleheader awaited in Philadelphia on the last stop.

Babe had given baseball his best, and although he was not up to playing those two final games, he donned his uniform one last time on May 30 for the twin bill in Baker Bowl. In his first at bat, he grounded out. Ruth seemed to wade in despair as he returned to the dugout and kept on going into the clubhouse. His ample shoulders bore the burden of a terrible truth.

Red Miller, the trainer, asked Babe if he needed help.

"No," Babe muttered. "There's nothing you can do for old age. I had too many good days to have it end on a bad day like this."

Except for a short-lived stint as a coach for the Brooklyn Dodgers in 1938, the magic ride was over. Babe's career had begun with a strikeout on July 11, 1914 and ended with a ground-out on May 30, 1935.

But what had transpired during the 21-year-span between those two at bats would never be equaled or forgotten.

After leaving baseball, Ruth lived quietly with Claire and their daughters in New York. Although he occasionally attended a game at Yankee Stadium where the crowd loudly cheered him, he existed on memories and the hope that some club would invite him to manage. "Babe would often sit by the phone, waiting for the call that never came," Claire later told a writer. "Sometimes when he couldn't take it any longer, he'd break down, put his head in his hands, and weep."

An overweight Babe faces the end of his career with the Braves in 1935.

In the cruelest twist of fate, baseball had turned its back on the Babe. But not the fans. They never forgot him and their adulation and constant stream of letters told Ruth how much they continued to adore the Bambino.

Reflecting on those painful days, Babe wrote in his autobiography, "It probably would have been easier if it hadn't been for the fans. From the mail I got—and always answered—and the receptions I had every place I went, and every place I drove or walked or flew, I felt that the public was as bewildered over my absence from baseball as I was."

On June 12, 1939, Babe was among the first group of immortals inducted into the Baseball Hall of Fame at Cooperstown. "You know," he told the audience, "for me this is just like an anniversary, because 25 years ago yesterday I pitched my first baseball game in Boston for the Boston Red Sox."

During the spring of 1939, Babe's friend and former teammate, Lou Gehrig, struggled during the early season with the Yankees. Medical

The Babe sits front and center among the game's first immortals at the initial induction ceremony at the Baseball Hall of Fame. Top, left to right: Honus Wagner, Grover Cleveland Alexander, Tris Speaker, Napoleon Lajoie, George Sisler, Walter Johnson. Bottom, left to right: Eddie Collins, Ruth, Connie Mack, Cy Young.

tests revealed that he was suffering from a fatal muscle disease called amyotrophic lateral sclerosis, which is now usually called "Lou Gehrig's Disease." On July 4, 1939, the Yankees honored Gehrig at ceremonies at Yankee Stadium. At the time of his retirement, Gehrig had established an unbelievable record of playing 2,130 consecutive games, earning the title of the "Iron Horse." Babe stood with his former Yankee teammates near one side of home plate as Gehrig stepped to the microphone.

In the late 1930s, Babe Ruth coached first base for the Brooklyn Dodgers. He always wanted to manage, and he was hurt that no one in baseball would give him a chance.

"I couldn't look at him when he began to talk," Babe remembered. "And when he said, 'I consider myself the luckiest man in the world,' I couldn't stand it any longer. I went over to him and put my arm around him, and though I tried to smile and cheer him up, I could not keep from crying."

Two months later, Adolf Hitler's German troops marched across Poland. The United States resisted being drawn into the approaching war, but when the Japanese bombed Pearl Harbor on December 7, 1941, America entered World War II. Although the 46-year-old Ruth was too old for military service, he supported the war effort by appearing in exhibition games and other special fund-raising events contributing to war charities.

In 1942, 69,136 fans filled Yankee Stadium for an Army-Navy Relief Fund Night. The Yankees asked Babe to appear. He would hit against one of the game's greatest pitchers, Walter Johnson. Before the exhibition, Babe was as excited as a busher making his first appearance in the big leagues.

At first, Babe teased the crowd by scattering 20 line drives around the same field where he had once sown his magic. But then the unmistakable crack was heard, instantaneously hushing the crowd. For a second, time seemed to stop as the fans watched in wonder, reliving the Ruthian miracle. The ball rose and arched and soared into the third deck of the right field stands. Then the stadium ignited in cheers that rose into the night, the sweet sound spilling into the streets of the Bronx.

Babe also promoted another cause very dear to him—America's youth and baseball. He established the Babe Ruth League for teenagers and actively supported the new group.

In November 1946, Babe experienced pain over his left eye. A malignant growth was discovered in the left side of his neck. Surgery removed the cancer and he received radiation treatments. It was obvious the Babe was seriously ill. He was extremely hoarse, his throat was constantly sore, and he lost 80 pounds.

Baseball Commissioner Happy Chandler declared that Sunday, April 27, 1947 would be Babe Ruth Day in the major leagues. Almost 60,000 fans filled Yankee Stadium to honor Ruth. Pale and thin, Babe walked on the field, dressed in his trademark camelhair coat and cap. As he stepped to the microphone to address the fans, his thoughts returned to the ceremonies honoring Lou Gehrig. Babe had told himself that such a tragedy could never happen again. "And yet I was destined to stand at the same home plate—only [eight] years later," Babe

Babe Ruth's last appearance at Yankee Stadium. He'd set 76 records during his career. Sixty-two still stood at his death.

wrote, "in much the same condition and under much the same circumstances."

Speaking in a raspy voice barely above a whisper, Babe spoke briefly to the crowd. "There have been so many lovely things said about me. I'm glad I can be here to thank everyone."

The day before the ceremonies, Babe had a special surprise. Johnny Sylvester, the crippled boy he had visited in the hospital in 1926, visited him. Sylvester had overcome his disease, attended Princeton, and was a Navy Lieutenant during World War II. "I'm grown up now, thanks to you," he told Babe. "And I figured it was only right for me to visit you, after your visit to me—a long time ago—did me so much good."

The doctors treated Babe's illness with experimental drugs and his health improved. With the help of writer Bob Considine, Ruth began writing his autobiography, which was published the following year. Sponsored by the Ford Motor Company, Babe also traveled the country on a promotional tour for American Legion Baseball. He established the Babe Ruth Foundation to help underprivileged children. In September 1947, the Yankees hosted an old-timers game to raise money for the cause. Babe watched as Ty Cobb, Tris Speaker and others played. "I was a spectator that day," Babe recalled. "Never enjoyed watching a game more than that one."

The following year, Ruth was well enough to attend the commemoration of the 25th anniversary of Yankee Stadium on June 13, 1948 at which time the club retired his number. The announcer called out his name. Wearing the pinstripes with the big 3 one last time, the frail Babe emerged from the dugout, a shadow of his former self. The crowd erupted. Amid the cheers, Ruth walked to the plate, steadying himself with a bat he used for a cane.

The cancer was in its final stages, but Babe fought on. "I honestly don't know anybody who wants to live more than I do," he wrote. "It is a driving wish that is always with me these days, a wish that only a person who has been near to death can know and understand."

In July he flew to his native Baltimore for an old-timers game. When it was rained out, Babe visited with his old friend and 1914 roommate, the writer Rodger Pippen, and the two reminisced about those long-ago days in Fayetteville.

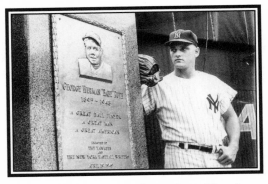

Roger Maris contemplates the tablet that for many years graced a memorial in Yankee Stadium's center field. It can now be seen in the stadium's memorial park. Maris hit 61 homers in 1961.

Ruth returned to New York where he entered the hospital. Despite his grave condition, he watched some of the first televised baseball games. His sister, Mamie Ruth Moberly, came to say good-bye to her brother. She found him extremely weak, but Babe greeted every visitor with the grin that was known all over the world. He listened intently as Claire read him countless letters from friends and fans.

Nothing in life had been able to contain the Babe: not a narrow rowhouse in Baltimore, an army of truant officers, the beatings of his father, nor frustrated baseball owners and managers. But even Babe's strong will could not conquer the cancer that took his life. He died in New York on August 16, 1948 at age 53.

The casket containing Ruth's body rested at Yankee Stadium where thousands of fans filed by to pay their final respects to the Babe. Francis Cardinal Spellman presided over the solemn requiem Mass in New York's St. Patrick's Cathedral on August 19.

Babe was laid to rest in the Gates of Heaven Cemetery in Hawthorne, New York.

Epilogue

No one made a greater impact on baseball than Babe Ruth. In many ways, he remained a child who inspired people throughout the world to embrace the childlike joy that is too often lost in that process known as "growing up." Babe had fun playing the game like no one else who ever put on spikes, and his legend endures today, a testimony to the lasting place he earned in our nation's history and in the hearts of Americans. And in that magical instant when the crack of the bat sends a ball soaring over the fence, in ballparks large and small, fans relive the wonder of baseball and remember George Herman "Babe" Ruth, the Sultan of Swat.

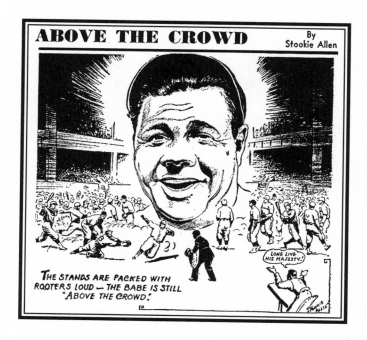

A Babe Ruth Chronology

February 6, 1895   Born in Baltimore, Maryland

June 13, 1902   Goes to live at St. Mary's Industrial School for Boys

February 1914   Signs with Baltimore Orioles of International League

July 10, 1914   Sold to Boston Red Sox

July 11, 1911   Wins first major league start, 4-3, over Cleveland

October 2, 1914   Gets first major league hit, a double

October 17, 1914   Marries Helen Woodford

May 6, 1915   Hits first major league home run

September 9, 1918   Sets World Series record, pitching 29-2/3 straight shutout innings

1919   Hits record 29 home runs and is converted to outfielder

112

January 5, 1920	Yankees announce purchase of Ruth from Red Sox
1920	Hits record 54 home runs
1921	Hits record 59 home runs
October 9, 1921	Hits his first World Series round-tripper
April 18, 1923	Hits home run in Opening Game at Yankee Stadium
October 6, 1926	Hits three home runs in one World Series game
September 30, 1927	Bests his own single-season record again with his 60th homer, setting a mark that would stand for 34 years
January 11, 1929	Helen Ruth dies in a fire
April 17, 1929	Marries Claire Hodgson
August 11, 1929	Hits 500th home run
August 21, 1931	Hits 600th home run
October 1, 1932	Beats Chicago Cubs in game 3 of the World Series with famed "Called Shot" home run
July 13, 1934	Hits 700th home run

February 1935	Yankees release Ruth and he signs with Boston Braves
May 25, 1935	Launches last three home runs at Pittsburgh for a lifetime total of 714
June 12, 1939	Inducted into the Baseball Hall of Fame in Cooperstown, New York
June 13, 1948	Makes final appearance in Yankee Stadium as Babe Ruth Day is celebrated in every major league ballpark
August 16, 1948	Dies of cancer in New York

The Babe's Statistical Record

Boston Red Sox, New York Yankees, Boston Braves

YEAR	TEAM	G	AB	R	H	2B	3B	HR	RBI	BA	SB
1914	BOS A	5	10	1	2	1	0	0	0	.200	0
1915		42	92	16	29	10	1	4	21	.315	0
1916		67	136	18	37	5	3	3	16	.272	0
1917		52	123	14	40	6	3	2	12	.325	0
1918		95	317	50	95	26	11	11	66	.300	6
1919		130	432	103	139	34	12	29	114	.322	7
1920	NY A	142	458	158	172	36	9	54	137	.376	14
1921		152	540	177	204	44	16	59	171	.378	17
1922		110	406	94	128	24	8	35	99	.315	2
1923		152	522	151	205	45	13	41	131	.393	17
1924		153	529	143	200	39	7	46	121	.378	9
1925		98	359	61	104	12	2	25	66	.290	2
1926		152	495	139	184	30	5	47	145	.372	11
1927		151	540	158	192	29	8	60	164	.356	7
1928		154	536	163	173	29	8	54	142	.323	4
1929		135	499	121	172	26	6	46	154	.345	5
1930		145	518	150	186	28	9	49	153	.359	10
1931		145	534	149	199	31	3	46	163	.373	5
1932		133	457	120	156	13	5	41	137	.341	2
1933		137	459	97	138	21	3	34	103	.301	4
1934		125	365	78	105	17	4	22	84	.288	1
1935	BOS N	28	72	13	13	0	0	6	12	.181	0
Total		2503	8399	2174	2873	506	136	714	2211	.342	123
World Series											
(10 Years)		41	129	37	42	5	2	15	33	.326	4
All-Star Games											
(2 Years)		2	6	2	2	0	0	1	2	.333	0

PITCHING STATISTICS

YEAR	TEAM	W	L	PCT	ERA	G	GS	CG	IP	H	BB	SO	ShO
1914	BOS A	2	1	.667	3.91	4	3	1	23	21	7	3	0
1915		18	8	.692	2.44	32	28	16	217.2	166	85	112	1
1916		23	12	.657	1.75	44	41	23	323.2	230	118	170	9
1917		24	13	.649	2.01	41	38	35	326.1	244	108	128	6
1918		13	7	.650	2.22	20	19	18	166.1	125	49	40	1
1919		9	5	.643	2.97	17	15	12	133.1	148	58	30	0
1920	NY A	1	0	1.000	4.50	1	1	0	4	3	2	0	0
1921		2	0	1.000	9.00	2	1	0	9	14	9	2	0
1930		1	0	1.000	3.00	1	1	1	9	11	2	3	0
1933		1	0	1.000	5.00	1	1	1	9	12	3	0	0
Total		94	46	.671	2.28	163	148	107	1221.1	974	441	488	17
World Series													
(2 Years)		3	0	1.000	0.87	3	3	2	31	19	10	8	1

Further Readings

Allen, Lee. *Babe Ruth: His Story in Baseball.* New York: G. P. Putnam, 1986.

Creamer, Robert. *Babe, The Legend Comes to Life.* New York: Simon & Schuster, 1974.

Eisenbery, Lisa. *The Story of Babe Ruth: Baseball's Greatest Legend.* New York: Dell-Yearing. 1990.

Macht, Norman. *Babe Ruth.* New York: Chelsea House, 1991.

Pirone, Dorothy Ruth. *My Dad the Babe: A Life in Pictures.* New York: Quinlan Press, 1988.

Ritter, Lawrence, and Mark Rucker. *The Babe: A Life in Pictures.* New York: Ticknor & Fields, 1988.

Ruth, Babe. *The Babe Ruth Story.* (As told to Bob Considine). New York: E. P. Dutton, 1948.

Video

Baseball: A Film by Ken Burns. Washington, DC. A Production of Florentine Films and WETA, 1994.

Acknowledgments

For their invaluable assistance with this book, the author wishes to thank Greg Schwalenberg, Curator of the Babe Ruth Museum, and Mark Rucker of Transcendental Graphics.

Photo Credits

Babe Ruth Museum: 16, 18, 21, 22, 26, 28, 30, 34, 36, 40, 42, 50, 55, 56, 85, 89, 92, 99, 100, 104, 108.

Bettmann Archives: 79, 83, 97.

Franklin Brittingham: 101.

National Baseball Library: 103.

Transcendental Graphics: 6, 9, 13, 15, 45, 46, 48, 60, 62, 65, 66, 69, 70, 73, 74, 76, 80, 82, 84, 86, 90, 91, 94, 98, 102, 105, 106, 110, 111.

Cover Photo: Baseball Card from the 1993 edition of The Sporting News ® Conlon Collection ™ reprinted with permission of Megacards, Inc., Fairfield, IA 52556 and The Sporting News Publishing Co., St. Louis, MO 63166. Babe Ruth reprinted with permission of Curtis Management Group, Indpls, IN., THE SPORTING NEWS ® and CONLON COLLECTION ™ and trademarks of The Sporting News Publishing Co.

Back Cover Photo: Transcendental Graphics.

Index